the end of suffering

the end of suffering
finding purpose in pain

SCOTT CAIRNS

PARACLETE PRESS
BREWSTER, MASSACHUSETTS

The End of Suffering: Finding Purpose in Pain

2009 First Printing

Copyright © 2009 by Scott Cairns
ISBN 978-1-55725-563-1

Library of Congress Cataloging-in-Publication Data

Cairns, Scott.
  The end of suffering : finding purpose in pain / Scott Cairns.
    p. cm.
  Includes bibliographical references.
  ISBN 978-1-55725-563-1
  1. Suffering--Religious aspects--Christianity. I. Title.
  BT732.7.C325 2009
  231'.8--dc22

                                        2009018728

10 9 8 7 6 5 4 3 2 1

Published by Paraclete Press
Brewster, Massachusetts
www.paracletepress.com
Printed in the United States of America

contents

The day itself is noticeably bitter, with a steady, blowing cold that makes my knuckles ache and my wet face numb as I bend to shovel more dirt from the heavy wheelbarrow onto our dogs' graves. We buried one Labrador in December, and a second in February. Mona was Leo's mother, and I called her the "mother of all Labradors." She went first. Leo followed, as he was wont to do. On this bleak day in March, I've noticed that the graves have settled some, and that is why I'm shoveling on more dirt.

———

It so happens that I have been puzzling over the ubiquity of grief and pain for a good while now— pretty much off and on since my father fell ill in the fall of 1985 and more continuously since he died of that long illness in the winter of 1988. I suppose that those years mark my conscious entry into the "valley of the shadow of death." In fact, I remember saying to my brother Steve—some weeks after witnessing our father's final throes—that I was having a hard time shaking free of a deep heaviness that kept weighing on me then.

I also recall that in those disquieting days I spoke of this heaviness as *dread*.

In any case, all of this is to say that like most people I, too, have been blindsided by personal grief now and again over the years. And I have an increasingly keen sense that, wherever I am, someone nearby is suffering now.

For that reason, I lately have settled in to mull the matter over, gathering my troubled wits to undertake a difficult essay, more like what we used to call an *assay,* really—an earnest inquiry. I am thinking of it just now as *a study* in suffering, by which I hope to find some sense in affliction, hoping—just as I have come to hope about experience in general—to *make something of it.*

Given affliction's generous availability, and given the wide, but so far unsatisfying, range of apologia that the nagging enigma of our human suffering has provoked over the years, I thought I might press ahead for a more satisfying glimpse of why it is we suffer, and why it is that some of us—even among the apparently innocent—appear to suffer far more than others.

At the very least, I would like to come up with a less specious way of talking about it.

———

I don't especially want to point fingers, but I am pretty sure that most of us have had our fill of the disturbing pieties that swirl about in the aftermath of suffering and loss, most of which strike me as being, at best, the unfortunate hybrids of good intentions and poor theology. And I am pretty sure that we would all like to feel less tongue-tied as we attempt to comfort a friend who has suffered a devastating loss.

Whenever I hear such commonplace yammerings as "God took him," "God needed her in heaven," or "we don't know why God would send us a hurricane," my heart registers a particularly heavy weight, and my dim wits teeter in chagrined incredulity.

I wouldn't say that my current purpose is all that Miltonic; that is, I don't feel compelled, exactly, to "justify the ways of God to man," but lately I do feel a pressing need to mitigate some of the nonsense that we habitually lay on the invisible God, presuming, as we seem to do, that He is the only one who has *acted* in every case.

That is to say, while I am nonetheless confident that He and His bodiless messengers have kept me and mine from harm, off and on, I am similarly confident that when harm does come to us, He is not necessarily the one who sent it.

His ways are not our ways—true enough—but I am not convinced that our every disaster or tragedy or accident is rightly attributed to be one of His inexplicable ways. It would be an added and very welcomed bonus not to feel myself tempted toward sin against the pastor every time I hear an ill-considered eulogy.

Finally, I would admit as well that my own faltering faith has come to demand a somewhat more satisfying take on this ubiquitous business of affliction.

The graves of two dogs may seem to some to be a relatively poor starting point—maybe even, to some, an insulting starting point—for this sort of inquiry. I hope not. I would never mean to equate the loss of a dog—or even the loss of two very good dogs—with every other occasion of human suffering. Still, I will not discount how hard, how sharp, even this loss remains—and how puzzling. It's the puzzlement, frankly, that makes even this current, specific grief remind me more generally of other grief, of other painful occasions, and of our overall predicament.

In any case, as I shovel and as I weep over my big sweet dogs, I wince off and on, a little embarrassed that in a world where each newscast and newspaper brings new images of heart-wrenching human tragedy, I continue to be so broken up over losing my dogs.

My only defense for the moment will have to be that these really were extraordinarily good dogs. And they loved me.

They were Labradors, no less.

Big yellow Labradors.

Innocent as rain.

the end of suffering

The end of suffering

one *waking up*

My heart is troubled; my strength fails me,
And the light of my eyes, even this is not with me.
—PSALM 37:11

I am guessing that it must have been fairly early in February of 2002 when I was first asked how the tragedy of September 11, 2001, had changed America. The young woman standing before me—my trembling and breathless interlocutor—appeared to be a fledgling student-reporter-on-the-street, and as she spoke I was thinking that she was asking her weighty question too lightly. Her self-conscious embarrassment and acute nervousness, in retrospect, were what had made her rush, what had made her nearly sing out her question, and probably what had made her smile as she did so.

Being accosted this way is par for our course here-abouts. I live in Columbia, Missouri, and thanks to a famous journalism school at the University of Missouri, ours is a modest town overrun with journalists, with professors of journalism, and with a largely giddy cohort of young men and women who are hoping to prepare—over the next four or so years—for gainful employment as print or television journalists. At the beginning of each semester, walking onto campus from the adjacent downtown can feel like running a gauntlet as the newbies try their hands at "doing journalism."

In any case, on this crisp February afternoon, a trembling young woman held a microphone to my mouth and stood waiting for my response. More specifically, she held the microphone at just about eye level, making it all but impossible for me to see her face as she spoke. Her hand—which I *did* see very vividly at the end of my nose—was shaking, and she seemed generally unsteady in what looked to be her new heels. Her partner, a gangly guy with something of a sophomore belly beneath a pea-green hooded sweatshirt, wore an orange stocking cap and sported multiple piercings in the one ear I could see; the rest of his face was hidden behind an oversized shoulder-cam, which also appeared to tremble some. As I have said, it was very early in the semester, and this may have been the rookie pair's first attempt at cold-calling a street corner interview.

Inexperienced as these two may have appeared, they nonetheless managed to snag me as I hurried back to campus after lunch, and they had opened with a question that—I suddenly realized—no one had actually asked me directly until that minute.

I stopped walking.

I stood, slack-jawed, puzzling how to answer them.

For a few mute seconds, I couldn't think of anything to say at all. And then it occurred to me to say something that I don't think I had fully acknowledged until I heard it come out of my mouth.

Of course, I had to tilt my head in order to see around the microphone and meet the young woman's eyes, but then I told her that I didn't think the tragedy of September 11 had changed our actual situation much at all; what it did, I supposed, was reveal how deeply mistaken our earnest illusions had been. The events of that day confronted us with an ongoing reality that—for many, many years—most Americans (and me included) had been content to ignore, even if it was also a reality that most folks in the world lived with on a daily basis.

"Hey, that's good," blurted the guy behind the shoulder-cam. He sounded genuinely surprised.

"Yeah, really," said the girl with the microphone, still smiling. "Like a wake-up call."

It was my turn to be surprised.

A wake-up call.

Precisely.

Now that I have had the chance to mull over these nagging matters with something in the neighborhood of deliberation, I'm thinking that this is what most, if not all, of our afflictions are inclined to do.

It is, at the very least, something that our afflictions are capable of doing.

They grab our attention.

They shake us up and, by thus rattling the bars of our various cages, they serve to shake us—blinking all the while—awake.

In this way, our afflictions oblige us to glimpse and to appreciate a somewhat bigger picture; they offer us a chance to see the greater, more troubling scope of our situation—the roiling reach of what, back in my own college days, we were fond of calling "the human condition."

And they help us to acknowledge the seriousness of that condition more deliberately than we may have felt obliged to do before affliction's painful occasion reared up, grabbed us by a tender ear, and bid us to attend to the lesson at hand.

In the case of 9/11, the event and our shock at it have come to illustrate for me a famous, particularly uncanny aphorism penned by the philosopher Simone Weil,[1] whose own life became something of a study in affliction, albeit affliction with a purpose. She writes: "Affliction compels us to recognize as real what we do not think possible."[2]

That is, our afflictions import a healthy dose of credence into our incredulity.

Which is to say that they have a chance of making believers of us.

Under most circumstances, then, the occasions of our suffering are capable of revealing what our habitual illusions often obscure, keeping us from knowing. Our afflictions drag us—more or less kicking—into a fresh and vivid awareness that we are not in control of our circumstances, that we are not quite whole, that our days are salted with affliction.

They insist on our noticing how our seasons move through cycles of joy and pain, and that our very lives—not to put too fine a point on it—are fairly (and sometimes unfairly) riddled with death.

_____

If we take care to acknowledge these truths, and are canny enough to attend to them, faithful enough to lean *into* them, then the particular ache of that waking can initiate a response that the Greeks were wont to call *kenosis*—an emptying, an efficacious *hollowing*.

Under ideal circumstances and duly appreciated, this hollowing can lead us into something of a *hallowing* as well.

These recognitions can lead us into some serious decentering—vertiginous and transforming moments. These also can become illuminating moments in which we see our lives in the context of a terrifying, abysmal *emptiness* (that would be the hollowing), moments when all of our comfortable assumptions are shown to be false, or misleading, or at least incomplete. They are shown to be downright insufficient.

If we are lucky,[3] an emptying like this can avail a glimpse of the somewhat broader view—the abysmal *fullness* in which "we live and move and have our being" (Acts 17:28).

This lucky realization would initiate what I will call our hallowing; and, as one might suppose, it can feel very much like a consolation—having transformed our painful, kenotic emptying into a *means* to a desirable end.

———

More than a hundred years ago, a chronically afflicted Emily Dickinson observed something of pain's curious effects and aftermath. "After great pain," she wrote, "a formal feeling comes." Her poem continues:

> The Nerves sit ceremonious, like Tombs—
> The stiff Heart questions 'was it He, that bore,'
> And 'Yesterday, or Centuries before'?
>
> The Feet, mechanical, go round—
> Of Ground, or Air, or Ought—
> A Wooden way
> Regardless grown,
> A Quartz contentment, like a stone—
>
> This is the Hour of Lead—
> Remembered, if outlived,
> As Freezing persons, recollect the Snow—
> First—Chill—then Stupor—then the letting go—[4]

In Dickinson's poem, the human person's experience of great pain is decidedly taken for granted; it is presented as *a given,* a patent and unavoidable circumstance. Also, it is figured—assuming that one survives it—as having passed.

The poem's attention focuses on what we—and the "Freezing persons" of the simile—are in the midst of this "chill" obliged to accept "the letting go."[5]

One might well think to ask, "The letting go of what?"

Very good question! And while I expect that we will make our way back to that very good question, for the moment, let's assume that the implication is apt—that we are all of us clinging to something.

Let's also assume that it might be to our common advantage to discover what that something is; let's also say that we might want to know *if* this habitual clinging of ours is helping our situation or hurting it.

Meantime, there are a great many ways to speak of pain's effects, lots of ways to appreciate its— what? Its purpose?

Maybe so.

Let's say yes.

One such way is offered up by Saint Isaac of Syria, a seventh-century saint who begins his observation by speaking of one particularly desirable outcome, and then—in a teacherly manner—proceeds to deduce for us how we are likely to find our way to it.

"The love of God," he writes, "proceeds from our conversing with Him; this conversation of prayer comes about through stillness, and stillness arrives with the stripping away of self."[6]

It would be good to notice the actual efficacious process that is in this way—albeit in reverse chronological order—presented: first occurs the stripping away of self, which produces a species of stillness, which avails actual prayer, which occasions the love of God.

If that particular phrasing, "the stripping away of self," strikes the contemporary ear as being a little painful, I am thinking that is probably because it most often is. The "stripping away of self" may also help to answer our very good question above, identifying what it is that we must be obliged to *let go*.

To be sure, I have stumbled upon a good bit of this business the hard way; but I am now supposing that this is the stubborn truth that has been nibbling my mind from the start—that the *hard way* is pretty much the only way most of us ever manage to learn anything.

Affliction, suffering, and pain are—even if they are nothing else—remarkably effective.

t w o *against self-esteem*

Why do you boast . . . O mighty man?
—PSALM 51:3

Among the slow—the apparently lifelong—lessons I seem to be catching on to, one significant discovery has to be the paradoxical, shooting-yourself-in-the-foot nature of self-interest, the self-defeating nature of self-regard. As you may remember, following the tragic madness and confusion of September 11, 2001, various angry and frightened American citizens responded in a startling variety of ways, supplying to our singular moment an *additional* tragic madness.

Among the more visible responses, we beheld earnestly patriotic gestures—a proliferation of American flags, impromptu rallies of solidarity, pathos-laden newspaper columns; these ranged from laudable expressions of empathy and of rediscovered community to less laudable, acutely disturbing expressions of rage directed at an invisible enemy. We witnessed, as well, no shortage of actual violence undertaken against citizens and against foreign visitors who had the bad luck of merely resembling those who had actually struck the blows against us.

Here in Columbia, Missouri, a much-beloved citizen—whose person and whose business happened to be named, respectively, Osama and Osama's— bore the brunt of some of this anxious patriotism—a broken storefront window, obscene graffiti, and racial slurs hollered by passing idiots.

Our little town was not unique. A Pakistani restaurant in Salt Lake City was set on fire in the night. A mosque in Allentown, Pennsylvania, was the target of a series of bomb threats that kept its community in turmoil and hunkered down anxiously for months. In Mesa, Arizona, Balbir Singh Sodhi, a Sikh, was shot to death as he pulled weeds in the garden outside his Chevron service station. Waquar Hasan, a Pakistani, was murdered in his downtown Dallas business, Mom's Grocery. The list goes on.

In the weeks following 9/11, the FBI opened 325 investigations into what were believed to be 9/11-related hate crimes. The Council on American-Islamic Relations received over 300 reports of harassment and violence during the 96 hours spanning Tuesday, September 11, and Friday,

September 14—nearly half the number it had received throughout the entire previous year.

The days following the attacks also delivered to American cars a self-conscious array of bumper stickers. One bumper sticker in particular caught my attention at the time, and has served in the interim to trouble my thoughts regarding our current state of affairs. It was a fairly simple—one might even say a *manifestly artless*—design: an American flag set in the center of a squat rectangle, framed by three words: *Faith. Hope. Pride.*

The word *Pride,* serving as the pedestal upon which the flag sat, was printed in slightly larger typeface and—perhaps not surprisingly—in bold.

Anyone with so much as a passing knowledge of the New Testament epistles probably could identify the text that had been so glibly revised into this curious new trinity of terms.

In the first of his letters to the young church in Corinth, Saint Paul writes:

> Though I speak with the tongues of men and of angels, but have not love, I have become sounding brass or a clanging cymbal. And though I have the gift of prophecy, and understand all mysteries and all knowledge, and though I have all faith, so that

I could remove mountains, but have not love, I am
nothing. And though I bestow all my goods to feed
the poor, and though I give my body to be burned,
but have not love, it profits me nothing.

The apostle concludes his observations on the
matter with these words: "And now abide faith,
hope, love, these three; but the greatest of these is
love" (1 Cor. 13:1–3, 13).

The bumper sticker of the moment had effectively
replaced the "greatest of these" with what—in a
more long-standing, moral economy—would be
recognized as a meager virtue at best, and which,
not all that long ago, would have been readily
recognized as chief among sins, if not their primary
cause.

How does such a curious evolution—such a
significant slippage—come about?

How is an essential sin recuperated into an
estimable virtue?

Why are those who speak of the power of their
pride so certain of their position? And why—one
might well ask—are they smiling?

This odd recuperation of *pride* has become in
recent years a commonplace. Earlier this fall, to
make room for a familiar fund-raising scheme,

the red brick and concrete walkway to our campus
alumni center was torn up and replaced with a span
of newer red bricks, each bearing the name of an
alumni center donor. Sections of red brick have
been separated by broad strips of granite, and each
of these is engraved with a single word.

For the most part, these words sport laudable
sentiments; most are at least benign: *Discovery,
Diversity, Respect, Responsibility,* and *Tradition.* The
presence of *tradition* strikes me as ironic, given that
etched there amid the other stony abstractions one
polished strip of granite offers—boldly and with
nary a qualm—*Pride.*

In an age that so insistently privileges
self-help, self-discovery, and—most troubling—
self-esteem, *pride* strikes many of us as a likely
path to liberation, freeing us from, say, oppressive
cultural biases, from dysfunctional families, and
from nagging self-doubt. As far as I can tell, it
appears to be our generation's best defense against
self-loathing, which is without question an even
greater sin.

From what I have gathered in recent years—as I
have observed the legion advocates of self-esteem
performing earnest interventions—I am pretty

sure that regardless of how much we advertise our ostensible pride, we appear mostly to be masking (none too convincingly) that same, pervasive self-loathing.

Methinks it smacks of our protesting too much.

I also suppose that when we childishly privilege our own self-aggrandizement, and when we—by so doing—cut ourselves off from our communities, both past and present, we are doomed to reinvent a fleet of troubled wheels, and, as the venerable Art Linkletter once observed about children in general, we "say the darnedest things."

It might be good for us to reconnect with our communal past, our shared traditions.

It certainly would be good to grow up.

————

Saint Isaac counsels, "Blessed is the person who knows his own weakness, because awareness of this becomes for him the foundation and the beginning of all that is good and beautiful."[7] Affliction appears to be our only reliable access to this kind of knowledge, this necessary confrontation with our own weaknesses, and this advantageous mitigation of our pride. And it seems to be the only way we come to glimpse and thereafter *to know* our condition, to appreciate our vulnerability, and to live according to this new and chastening light.

I have come to think of this knowledge as an efficacious and corrective tilt of the head, an opportunity to see what I previously had not been prepared to see. More than that, it may compel me to see what I, subconsciously, had worked very hard *not* to see.

If we were to take greater advantage of these suddenly new perspectives, we might appreciate affliction as *the foundation of the foundation, the beginning of the beginning*—as Saint Isaac has presented it—"of all that is good and beautiful," but that is assuming we manage to respond *well* to these our afflictions, responding alertly, seriously, humbly, and in good faith.

I have a strong sense that most of us, most of the time, do respond fairly well—at least to our own suffering. Still, even if that is the case, I am now beginning to suspect that this more or less *local* focus may not be enough.

Faced with personal affliction, immediate pain—the prospect of cancer, or heart disease, or the heartrending loss of someone we love—most of us respond wisely, with something like a chastened, sober, more circumspect life. I remember the words of a wise monk I happened to meet very briefly on Mount Athos near the end of his life; he was fully aware that he was dying of cancer, and had once comforted his (and my) beloved friend Stelios by saying to him that "paradise is filled with men and women whose cancer saved their lives."

This is quite a radical perspective, no?

Shocking as his words may sound to us nowadays, I am inclined to think that the Athonite father had an uncommonly keen sense of certain facts that most of us dimly apprehend. While we may be tempted to respond to such final pains with bitterness, disappointment, and resentment, I've personally known dozens who have seized this opportunity to become the men and women that they had, in their deepest hearts, long desired to be.

It was as if their imminent deaths freed them *from* petty, distracted lives, and freed them *into* greater, genuine living—however briefly.

Addressing the fact of his own terminal cancer, writer Raymond Carver left the following observation in a very late poem called "Gravy." Despite the dire and daunting circumstances that his poem effectively catalogs, a deep base note of joy resounds throughout these lines. The choice of third-person point-of-view itself may even manifest a subtle, attractive species of "letting go," a calm and ready "stripping away of self."

> No other word will do. For that's what it was. Gravy.
> Gravy, these past ten years.
> Alive, sober, working, loving and
> being loved by a good woman. Eleven years
> ago he was told he had six months to live
> at the rate he was going. And he was going
> nowhere but down. So he changed his ways
> somehow. He quit drinking! And the rest?
> After that it was all gravy, every minute
> of it, up to and including when he was told about,
> well, some things that were breaking down and
> building up inside his head. "Don't weep for me,"
> he said to his friends. "I'm a lucky man.
> I've had ten years longer than I or anyone
> expected. Pure gravy. And don't forget it."[8]

My own father was a man whose frenetic creative activities kept him moving from one art form to another throughout his life. He was also a man who—like the son writing this—was prone to impatience and had struggled over years to rein in a considerable temper. During his last years, as the cancer in his throat commenced to spread throughout the rest of his body, my father became a remarkably calm, loving, and profoundly quiet man; he became—I now realize—a genuine man of prayer.

During the days immediately following his death, my mother said to me, "A lot of people—when they know they're dying—get angry and bitter; your father just got sweeter." Of the countless lessons my father taught me during our thirty-four years together—a time that seems all too brief—this was the most significant: how to die, how to die well.

In my experience, this is not such an uncommon phenomenon among people of faith—the ability to discover the uncanny blessing in the midst of our own suffering, our own pain. It makes evident what Saint Paul identified as "the peace of God, which surpasses all understanding" (Phil. 4:7).

Faced with the pain of others, however, some of us are tempted to respond less well.

In his famous poem, "Musée des Beaux Arts," W.H. Auden writes:

> About suffering they were never wrong,
> The Old Masters; how well, they understood
> Its human position; how it takes place

While someone else is eating or opening a window
        or just walking dully along;
How, when the agéd are reverently,
        passionately waiting
For the miraculous birth, there always must be
Children who did not specially want it to happen,
        skating
On a pond at the edge of the wood:
They never forgot
That even the dreadful martyrdom must
        run its course
Anyhow in a corner, some untidy spot
Where the dogs go on with their doggy life and
        the torturer's horse
Scratches its innocent behind on a tree.
In Breughel's Icarus, for instance: how everything
        turns away
Quite leisurely from the disaster;
        the ploughman may
Have heard the splash, the forsaken cry,
But for him it was not an important failure;
        the sun shone
As it had to on the white legs disappearing
        into the green
Water; and the expensive delicate ship that
        must have seen
Something amazing, a boy falling out of the sky,
had somewhere to get to and sailed calmly on.[9]

I have called this long essay *The* End *of Suffering*.
By so doing I hope to double-up on the connotations
of that suggestive word, *end*. Certainly, I mean to
gesture toward a someday conclusion—a day when
suffering will be no more, when, as the Scriptures
indicate, "there shall be no more death, nor sorrow,
nor crying" (Rev. 21:4)—but, more than that, I
hope to invoke in this our puzzling *mean*time a
sense of suffering's *purpose,* to imply what each of
us suspects: that suffering is no end in itself, and
that affliction is, of itself, no great virtue.

That said, then, we must come to recognize our
suffering as a *means,* a circumstance of our common
journey that can offer us a clearer view of the task
at hand. Along that journey, our afflictions and our
suffering may also provide to us a glimpse of what
actual virtue might require.

three *one body, his*

In the midst of the church I will sing to You.
—PSALM 21:23

Writers and other artists are sometimes prone to isolation, and in that isolation, we are likely to feel varying degrees of alienation from our communities—so much so, we may also feel justified in self-centeredness, even if it seems to us more like self-preservation or self-defense.

However it may feel or seem, and however we may justify it, this disconnect from those around us is not, of itself, a good thing—though it may, off and on, lead to a good thing.

Some four years ago, I joined a very likely crew of art-friendly, art-engaged folk to take part in one of the annual workshops sponsored by *Image* journal and its sponsoring agency, the Center for Religious Humanism. While gatherings like these can offer an immediate remedy for the artist's isolation, they also provide a sense that our reconnecting to *each other* is necessary for our becoming individually whole.

From my first glance at the program for the week, I was intrigued that Greg Wolfe and his staff had chosen to tag that year's gathering with the theme of "Love and Affliction."

We were, by that curious juxtaposition, confronted with a number of complexities that I, for one, had overlooked. Specifically, I was nudged into seeing that my own habitual sense of isolation—duly considered—might take on a spiritual dimension; with the pairing of *love* and *affliction,* I was invited to think of my own discomfort as a discipline, even an ascetic discipline, and a means to an end— something, that is, that I might *work through*.

And I was reminded that love itself is often manifested in our paying attention, by our giving care; I was reminded that, in the case of art making, this is often performed by our giving great care to the *stuff* of creation. I was also intrigued that the theme had identified the challenging paradox of our shared impulse to create art even in the face of suffering. This was a provocative pairing, suggesting that our *taking pains* to make *anything* well could be understood, in one sense, as a consolation for things around us that appear to be poorly fashioned.

Any well-made thing—whether held in the hand or viewed from afar—stands in stark contrast to the shoddy around us: a manifestly disastrous economic system, for instance, or criminal corporate strategies and structures, or cyclical erosions of our political and legal institutions, or—just so you don't think I'm simply pointing fingers here—the chagrin of our own faltering, sputtering lives, dissipated in self-defeating habits and distractions.

Good art *is* something of a consolation; good art is potentially something more—bearing what might turn out to be a *corrective,* a *remedial* agency.

Good art certainly serves as a consolation for those relatively few who make it, especially for those exceptional folk who struggle to make it well. Laboring over the wheel, the canvas, the written page, or the musical score can bring to the laborer a powerfully consoling sense of purpose. The literary critic and philosopher George Steiner indicates a helpful sense of why this is so:

> Any coherent understanding of what language is and how language performs, . . . any coherent account of the capacity of human speech to communicate meanings and feeling is, in the final

analysis, underwritten by the assumption of God's presence. I will put forward the argument that the experience of aesthetic meaning in particular, that of literature, of the arts, of musical forms, infers the necessary possibility of this "real presence." The seeming paradox of a "necessary possibility" is, very precisely, that which the poem, the painting, the musical composition are at liberty to explore and enact. This study will contend that the wager on the meaning of meaning . . . is a wager on transcendence.[10]

Personally, I am not exactly a big fan of "transcendence," because it sometimes attests to a disposition of *spiritual* fervor that tends to discount the material world and its bouquets of lovely stuff, in favor of the immaterial.

Our specifically Christian undertaking is decidedly not one of *transcending*. It is, rather, the intentional reinspiriting of the body and its lowly matter—as manifested in the incarnation of Christ.

Fortunately, this glib dismissal of the body is *not* what the wise Mr. Steiner is after; rather, he is advocating that our significance—and predilection for signifying—has to do with an implicit relationship to the Real—a Real that is beyond us. I prefer to consider the Real as being both beyond us and, by God's grace, increasingly within us.

In an earlier book, *Tolstoy or Dostoevsky,* Steiner puts the matter more explicitly yet: "A Pascalian wager on the transcendent is the essential foundation for the understanding of language, for the ascription of meaning to meaning. This wager, moreover, implicitly or explicitly characterizes major art and literature from Homer and Aeschylus almost to the present; it alone allows us to 'make sense' of music."[11] For Steiner, then, the act of making art, of writing literature, and of composing music demonstrates an implicit expectation of a reality that abides beyond (and perhaps within) what is apparent, a reality that provides the necessary context for *any* significance, *any* meaning making.

For the artist of any art, therefore, it is not surprising that these labors can provide a deeply satisfying consolation, giving witness to one's own subconscious hope, one's own implicit—avowed or disavowed—faith.

Beyond this local benefit to the artist himself, good art can offer more generally a consolation to all of those who have labored to *receive* it well. The quiet calm that accompanies our hours in the museum, the gallery, the studio, the concert hall—where we "'make sense' of music"—is, at the very least, consoling.

A *well-made thing well received* quietly suggests that all things we undertake to accomplish be undertaken with care; in this way, the *well-made thing* bears an undeniable power to affect us and to enhance our expectations; it nudges us to raise the bar.

To the extent that the *well-made thing* provokes a responsive, corrective self-examination, it works concurrently to educe from us our ongoing, active, and answering creation—an answer that manifests our desire for wholeness and reconciliation. One might say that, in attending to such art and in answering it with substantive response, we *make our hope matter*.

More generally, to the extent that this practice teaches us simply to honor *care taken,* it also teaches us to be a good deal less content with the shabby, the hasty, the thoughtless, the narrow, and the glib. Our learning to honor the serious labor that goes into a well-made artifact might—if we make the expansive connection—teaches us to honor the serious labor involved in shaping a well-made life.

We might even be tempted to get busy shaping one.

We may not choose our afflictions, but we do choose what to make of them.

Earlier, I offered "Musée des Beaux Arts" by W.H. Auden. Its ambivalences and edgy ironies provide a clue to the dark heart of our trouble—namely, what keeps us separate, severed, and self-absorbed is a habitual disinclination to take seriously the suffering of others.

In Auden's words, the failures and travails of others do not often strike us as "important failures." Like his poem's busy plowman, the dog absorbed by doggy life, the executioner's itchy horse, like the pretty ship with somewhere else to go, we too seldom *partake in* the failing and the suffering of our various members, and we therefore fail to realize the fullness, the reality, the appalling mystery of life as One Body. Simply put, I am now supposing that until we come to recognize everyone's failure as a personal failure, we are unlikely ever to succeed as we must.

———

During a deliciously sweet span of two or so years—thanks to a research leave from my university and the beneficence of the Guggenheim Foundation—I was able to enjoy a series of extended visits to Mount Athos, a unique region of northern Greece known also as Agion Oros, "the Holy Mountain." I continue to think of my journeys there as pilgrimages, expeditions into something of a *new* world—even if the world of Mount Athos may seem to be the odd vestige of a very *old* world. I hope—God willing—to make return visits to the holy enclaves of the fathers throughout my life, which I have come to understand as one continuing pilgrimage.

Initially, I journeyed to the Holy Mountain for guidance toward what is traditionally called *interior prayer,* or the *prayer of the heart.* That is to say, so I might better learn to pray, and—not to put too fine or too grand a point on it—to do so ceaselessly. While I may have picked up a thing or two about the practice of prayer during my time with the monks and their mountain, I learned something else as well; I like to think of it as a bonus.

I learned—from firsthand encounter with contemporary ascetics—a little bit about affliction. And I learned an additional bit about its unexpected benefits.

Moreover, I realized—*experienced,* even—that the body of Christ is a good deal more than a figure of speech; it is an appalling truth and mystery, uniting us beyond our knowing with one another, and uniting us with an ever-greater mystery, the *perichóresis*—the circling dance—of the Holy Trinity Who is our One God.

I do not expect to comprehend—much less ever to explain—the particular mystery of, as I come to speak of it, *One Holy Essence Whose Mystery is expressed in relational, interpersonal terms,* but I do hope to share something glimpsed among the struggling monks on their Holy Mountain, something gleaned from their ongoing, written tradition, and something I have labored to acquire as my own.

I have spoken the words, "the body of Christ," for decades without thinking much about what those words demand. Lately, I have seen how our greater awareness *of* and our intentional performance *as* the mystical body of Christ might assist in our apprehension of suffering's purpose, as well as its end.

Saint Symeon the New Theologian, writing in the tenth century, offers his own firsthand experience of one amazing aspect—one *face,* we might say—of our neglected mystery when he writes of Christ:

He was suddenly completely there,
united with me in an ineffable manner,
joined to me in an unspeakable way
and immersed in me without mixing
as the fire melds as one with the iron,
and the light with the crystal.
And He made me as though I were all fire.
And He showed me myself as light
and I became that which before me I saw
and I had contemplated only from afar.
I do not know how to express to you
the paradox of this manner.
For I was unable to know
and I still now do not know
how He entered, how He united Himself with me.[12]

Through the mystery of God's grace, we are united with Christ. As Saint Paul writes, mystically we "*put on* Christ,"[13] adopting His holiness as He adopts our humanity. This is astonishing, but it is something that most of us have no trouble affirming.

From what I have gathered over the years, we appear to have so little trouble affirming it that we seldom bother even to think of it, much less to consider its vertiginous implications. Oblivious as fatted cattle munching a numbing cud, we are likely to squander an inestimable gift, unawares.

We are, in no uncertain terms, called to be *like Christ,* and if we will choose to allow it, we will grow into His holy likeness, increasingly and forever. The fact that His holiness is unending and inexhaustible means that each of us has an exhilarating and endless journey ahead.

Even so—and more to the point of the difficult moment—we often neglect how, if this delicious mystery should apply to our own beloved persons, it necessarily must apply to other persons as well.

Nearly always, when puzzling over that mystery—the church as Christ's body—I find my thoughts returning to a particularly famous provocation in Saint Matthew's Gospel, where Christ informs his followers, "Inasmuch as you did it to one of the least of these my brethren, you did it to Me."

This passage, as it happens, is read during Orthodox liturgy on the morning of every "Meat Fare" Sunday—the day just prior to the church's preparations for the Lenten fast. The lectionary insists that this Gospel passage be read at this time, encouraging parishioners to keep their eyes on the purpose of the fast rather than on its legal terms. Fasting should assist our becoming a community of men and women who witness—by their lives in

Christ—a mystical union with Him and with all others.

This stunning observation regarding Christ's being identified with His people—with every one of them—occurs in the final parable among a good many that Christ speaks to His disciples on the Mount of Olives, laboring to introduce those perplexed followers to what will become their new lives *in Him*; the radically revisionary passage, in its entirety, is worthy of our continued close attention, word by word:

> Then the King will say to those on His right hand, "Come, you blessed of My Father, inherit the kingdom prepared for you from the foundation of the world: for I was hungry and you gave Me food; I was thirsty and you gave Me drink; I was a stranger and you took Me in; I was naked and you clothed Me; I was sick and you visited Me; I was in prison and you came to Me."
>
> Then the righteous will answer Him, saying, "Lord, when did we see You hungry and feed You, or thirsty and give You drink? When did we see You a stranger and take You in, or naked and clothe You? Or when did we see You sick, or in prison, and come to You?"

And the King will answer and say to them,
"Assuredly, I say to you, inasmuch as you did it
to one of the least of these My brethren, you did
to Me."

As appalling mysteries go, this one ranks among
the most appalling and most radical, being every bit
as terrible as it is beautiful. Its corollary is no less so:

Then He will also say to those on the left hand,
"Depart from Me, you cursed, into the everlasting
fire prepared for the devil and his angels: for I was
hungry and you gave Me no food; I was thirsty and
you gave Me no drink; I was a stranger and you did
not take Me in, naked and you did not clothe Me,
sick and in prison and you did not visit Me."

Then they also will answer Him, saying, "Lord,
when did we see You hungry or thirsty or a stranger
or naked or sick or in prison, and did not minister
to You? "

Then He will answer them, saying, "Assuredly, I
say to you, inasmuch as you did not do it to one of
the least of these, you did not do it to Me." (Mt.
25:34–45)

Our familiar English word *atonement*[14] (which,
believe it or not, comes of combining *at-one-ment*)

was coined in the sixteenth century for the express purpose of reinfusing our theologies with a more vivid awareness of *how* it is that Christ saves us— He joins Himself to us.

As much as we may like to speak of this union, and as much as we continue, week after week, to affirm it—whether we choose to offer that affirmation in our creeds or in the midst of our yammering doctrinal propositions—this mystery of our partaking of Christ's person is not a mystery that we (and here I am speaking mostly for myself) manage consistently either to embody or to perform.

Moreover, there remains one additional aspect of our being *the body of Christ* that garners even less of our attention. I'm referring to our being the *One* Body, or, as my friend the poet Li Young Lee has said it, "There is just the one body—nothing is unrelated to the whole."

That we are—each and all of us—mystically participant in the Holy Trinity through our partaking of Christ is but one face of the revolutionary shift occasioned by the Lord's Incarnation; we are also thereby mystically united to each other, whether we like it or not.

I'm not sure that I mean this in precisely the same way that my Taoist friend means it, but my hope is that we will *all* come to mean it more than we currently appear to. Finally, I am hoping that we may learn to act on it as well.

four *others as ourselves*

O Lord, I love the beauty of Your house,
and the place where Your glory dwells.
—PSALM 25:8

For the past twelve years or so, I have made a practice of saying the Jesus Prayer, which— give or take a few words—goes like so: "Lord Jesus Christ, Son of God, have mercy on me."

The prayer is a central practice within a long-standing and much revered Christian tradition of "stillness" and "watchfulness" that remains widespread throughout the Eastern church. It has become increasingly observed in the Western church, where Christians have become intentional about recovering the fullness of our common faith—an enriching fullness and a wholeness, which due to largely historical circumstances has been kept from a good many of us.

As a singular, thoughtful prayer, these words encourage the one who speaks them to attend deliberately to God's presence, here and now. As a continuing practice, they enable the one who repeats them (that is to say, the one who thereby acquires "the prayer of the heart") to hold on to that sense of His unfailing presence, always. The heart is, after all, God's "habitation," and the very locus "where His glory dwells"; in the Jesus Prayer, we learn to know this, to savor its truth, and to benefit from the spiritual growth that this dynamic mystery offers us.

For all our good intentions, our long-distracted crew—the ostensible followers of Christ—have squandered our diverse gifts over the centuries. We have even intermittently modified our theologies—lowering the bar of our expectations—time and time again to accommodate our failure to become what we are called to become. "No one is perfect," we repeat, smiling as we scribble our own doctor's excuse for the teacher.

Quoting the Hebrew Bible,[15] Saint Peter disagrees, and he reminds us of the ambitious measure we've been given for where the bar ought to be placed:

> Therefore, gird up the loins of your mind, be sober, and rest your hope fully upon the grace that is to be brought to you at the revelation of Jesus Christ; as obedient children, not conforming yourselves to the former lusts, as in your ignorance; but as He

who called you is holy, you also be holy in all your
conduct, because it is written, "Be holy; for I am
holy." (1 Pet. 1:13–16)

In the Greek, the exhortation is all the more
emphatic, "Holy you will be, because I am Holy."[16]
Gradually, through the prayer of the heart—by the
precious *gift* of this prayer—we come to apprehend
that our loving God is never *not* utterly near. And
we finally come to realize that on those occasions
when He seems to us to be far away, that numbing
circumstance *inevitably* has much more to do with
our own dim wits than it has to do with His having
withheld His availability. That is to say, *He* never
withdraws from *us*, but we—through volition or
through neglect—often withdraw from Him, and
thereby cloud our own intuitive senses.

For many of those twelve years that I have
practiced the prayer thus far, I have, off and on,
thought to replace the *me* of the prayer with *us,*
repeating "Lord Jesus Christ, have mercy on
us." I had imagined that by thus changing the
ancient prayer, I was petitioning for others in a
more intentional way. The obvious arrogance of
presuming to improve upon a beautiful and ancient
tradition aside, this modification did not seem at

first to be such a bad thing. Besides, when talking
about the practice some years ago, a Presbyterian
friend confessed that while she, too, was drawn to
the practice of the Jesus prayer, she had a difficult
time repeating *have mercy on me*. "It just seems a
little selfish," she said.

I had often felt the same way, and my modification
of the prayer was my response to uneasiness about
being overly self-concerned.

More recently, however, I have had occasion to
rethink the matter. I have come to the conclusion
that my innovative modification of the ancient
prayer[17] was actually a subtle refusal or maybe just
an acute ignorance of the facts I'm hoping now to
recover. It was an inadvertent denial of my mystical
relationship to other members of the body of
Christ—by which I now mean *all of them*.

As you might suppose, I didn't manage to puzzle
out any of this on my own, but was nudged into
the realization by a passage I found in *Wounded by
Love*, a beautiful book presenting the wisdom of
Elder Porphyrios of the Holy Mountain. "Pray for
others more than for yourself," says the Elder. "Say,
'Lord Jesus Christ, have mercy on me,' and you will
always have others in your mind. We are all children

of the same Father; we are all one. And so, when
we pray for others, we say 'Lord Jesus Christ, have
mercy on me,' and not, 'have mercy on them.' In
this way we make them one with ourselves."[18]

There is another, more subtle lesson lurking here
as well. Every time we decide unilaterally and unduly
to "change up" our received traditions, we are likely
to risk missing out on how those very traditions
might have helped us along the way. That is to say,
if we are too quick to reshape those traditions to suit
our immediate and individual tastes, we may never
know how those traditions might have reshaped
us, how they might have efficaciously availed for
us a more likely understanding of what we might
become.

I love how G.K. Chesterton suggests the logic of
this particular dynamic in his classic book *Orthodoxy.*
He does so with no shortage of accustomed, Chester-
tonian wit and humor:

> I have never been able to understand where people
> got the idea that democracy was is some way opposed
> to tradition. It is obvious that tradition is only
> democracy extended through time. It is trusting to
> a consensus of common human voices rather than to
> some isolated or arbitrary record. The man who quotes

some German historian against the tradition of the
Catholic Church, for instance, is strictly appealing to
aristocracy. He is appealing to the superiority of one
expert against the awful authority of a mob. It is quite
easy to see why a legend is treated, and ought to be
treated, more respectfully that a book of history. The
legend is generally made by the majority of people
in the village, who are sane. The book is generally
written by the one man in the village who is mad.
. . . Tradition may be defined as an extension of the
franchise. Tradition means giving votes to the most
obscure of all classes, our ancestors.[19]

As for the specific tradition of the Jesus Prayer, I
am now thinking that even if one were to initially
begin one's practice of the prayer by repeating "have
mercy on *us,*" the purpose at the very heart of our
matter is to realize how utterly we are connected
to those we love, to those for whom we pray. Their
well-being and our own should be so inextricably
connected that we apprehend how they are all—
every one of them—included in our saying "have
mercy on *me.*" Thereafter (though one surely cannot
rush this sort of thing) we may begin to suspect
next how all of Christ's body, all of humanity,
and—ultimately—all of creation are invoked in our
petition as well.

As for the current *me*? I'm still working on it.

It is one thing to agree with the mystery of our unity as a proposition, but something else to manifest that difficult matter with our lives.[20] To grasp and sustain an awareness of this intimate connection with others is perhaps our greatest human challenge. I know that it continues to be mine.

———

While it may not count as a "spiritual" practice, for the past fifteen years, I've made a habit of rereading Dostoevsky's *The Brothers Karamazov* during the summertime. For all the times that I have read through it, I continue to see that there remains more to the book than I have so far gathered. Call me a slow learner.

Generally, in late May, when administrative and teaching duties have concluded for the year and university life is winding down for the summer, I take up that weighty Russian novel for another go. For the most part, I manage to move through it steadily enough, except for the several passages having to do with Elder Zosimas, where I prefer to proceed slowly, deliberately, with increased attention to every word, and ever on the lookout for further illuminating connotation.

Of course, the entirety of Dostoevsky's novel
is reliably rich and suggestive, but those specific
passages in which the character Elder Zosimas[21]
speak at length are especially worthy of close
reading. They are unfailingly rewarding of repeated
visits. Initially, I had little clue about why this
book—and those passages—held so much power
for me; I only knew that they always did. I only
knew that the book always took me to another
discovery every time I picked it up. It wasn't until
some three or four years into my habit that I finally
noticed how powerfully present Saint Isaac of Syria
is in Dostoevsky's work. It is commonly known
that Dostoevsky kept his own copy of Saint Isaac's
Ascetical Homilies readily at hand and pored over
the text throughout his life.

Coincidentally, many years ago, as I was making
my own admittedly slow way toward the Eastern
church, it was Saint Isaac's *Homilies* that helped
to tug my heart home. As a result of that leading,
I thereafter took Saint Isaac as my "name saint"
when I was received into the Orthodox Church in
1998.

One passage in the saint's homilies that proved
especially helpful then—and now, as we puzzle

over this enigma of affliction—is this portion from the recently discovered "second part" of the saint's ancient text:

> [Both] the Kingdom and Gehenna are matters belonging to mercy. . . . That we should say or think that the matter [of Gehenna] is not full of love and mingled with compassion would be an opinion full of blasphemy and insult to our Lord God. . . . Among all His actions there is none which is not entirely a matter of mercy, love, and compassion: this constitutes the beginning and the end of His dealings with us.[22]

All of God's actions, the saint continues to insist, have to do with our recovery, with our becoming whole. None of His actions—not one—is unrelated to the overarching mercy, love, and compassion He bears for us. As the psalmist says, "The Lord chastened and corrected me, but He did not give me up to death" (Ps. 117:18). As the psalmist says, "He will not become angry to the end, Nor will He be wrathful forever";

> He did not deal with us according to our sins,
> Nor reward us according to our transgressions;
> For according to the height of heaven from earth,
> So the Lord reigns in mercy over those who fear Him;

As far as the east is from the west,
So He removes our transgressions from us. (Ps.
102:9–12)

For Isaac, then—and for me—even Gehenna is
finally understood to be remedial; it is understood
as a means to our recovery and not an end in itself—
never an end in itself.

In *The Brothers Karamazov,* our Saint Isaac is
mentioned by name several times, and the saint's
Ascetical Homilies acknowledged twice.

We are told that the servant Grigory kept a copy:
"[Grigory] loved the Book of Job,[23] and somewhere
obtained a copy of the homilies and sermons of
'Our God-bearing Father, Isaac the Syrian,' which
he read persistently over many years, understanding
almost nothing at all of it. . . ."[24]

Later, we witness—through the feverish eyes
of Ivan Karamazov on the eve of his own life-
threatening illness—that the scoundrel Smerdyakov
is also in possession of a copy (perhaps the same
copy, pilfered from Grigory). This is the last we see
of that malformed man—just prior to his taking his
own life.

While Grigory and Smerdyakov held these
homilies in hand, it is the Elder Zosimas who

appears to carry Saint Isaac's words written upon his heart; he is the one who is able to recall the saint's words and to incorporate them into his own speech, and—more to our point of the moment—he is the one who appears to have found a way to perform those words. That is to say, the Elder Zosimas has found a way to live *into* them.

During his one and only meeting with Dmitri Karamazov, the elder surprises all present with his sudden actions:

> [Zosimas] stepped towards Dmitri Fyodorovich and, having come close to him, knelt before him. Alyosha thought for a moment that he had fallen from weakness, but it was something else. Kneeling in front of Dmitri Fyodorovich, the elder bowed down at his feet with a full, distinct, conscious bow, and even touched the floor with his forehead. Alyosha was so amazed that he failed to support him as he got to his feet. A weak smile barely glimmered on his lips.
> "Forgive me! Forgive me, all of you!" he said, bowing on all sides to his guests.[25]

Soon thereafter, the elder, as he prepares to die, offers some late counsel to his brothers. "Love animals, love plants, love each thing," he entreats them.

"If you love each thing, you will perceive the mystery of God in things. Once you have perceived it, you will begin tirelessly to perceive more and more of it every day. And you will come at last to love the whole world with an entire, universal love."[26]

Elsewhere—as it happens, paraphrasing Saint Isaac—he avers:

> Remember also: every day and whenever you can, repeat within yourself: "Lord, have mercy upon all who come before you today." For every hour and every moment thousands of people leave their life on this earth, and their souls come before the Lord—and so many of them part this earth in isolation, unknown to anyone, in sadness and sorrow that no one will mourn for them, or even know whether they had lived or not. And so, perhaps from the other end of the earth, your prayer for his repose will rise up to the Lord, though you did not know him at all, nor he you. How moving it is for his soul, coming in fear before the Lord, to feel at that moment that someone is praying for him, too, that there is still a human being on earth who loves him.[27]

This is not as uncommon a disposition as we might suppose, radical as it appears to us in the habitual isolations of the twenty-first century.

Still, even today, the monks of Mount Athos and the monks and nuns throughout the world are intentional in living this mystery of our mystical unity and of our mutual responsibility—keen on actually living *into* it. With wholehearted struggle, they bear one another's afflictions—both physical and spiritual. With wholehearted struggle, they lift one another in prayer. With wholehearted struggle, they ask forgiveness for their personal sins, for those of their brothers, and—puzzling as this may seem to us—they ask God to forgive them for our sins as well.

One of the great and continuing misconceptions about monasticism past and present is that these men and women have withdrawn from—have rejected—the world altogether, and that by doing so they are primarily concerned with their own spiritual well-being, attending to their own "salvation," merely.

That may well be how their curious choice appears to us from *outside* their enclaves. From the inside, however, one can witness something more nearly true. Imitating Christ, they are—in daily and deliberate acts—performing the greatest love of all, that of giving their lives for their friends.

Granted, these men and women are laboring to apprehend their own salvation, but as their ascetic lives develop, their labors and their most earnest prayers are for the salvation of the entire world, for all of creation.

The modern Athonite Elder Porphyrios, then, does not stand alone in this insistence upon our implicit unity. Virtually all of the monks of Mount Athos struggle to acquire this understanding, along with increasing numbers of Christians worldwide who have worked to recover what has been for the most part a lost—one might dare even to say a *squandered*—tradition. These men and women have come to accept and to act upon the fact that, as members of the body of Christ, each of us is utterly responsible for every other member, and, as human persons, each is responsible for all of the sin and for all of the resulting suffering that come into the world.

For all of their apparent separation from "the world" and its madding crowd, these monks are paradoxically more attentive to its troubles than the majority of us who remain attached *to* and enamored *of* that world. While many of us manage to live in heart-numbing isolation even in the midst of a teeming city, certain of these ascetics—in their distant enclaves or in their solitary caves—continue to live in deliberate communion with each other and with all of humankind. And, unlike the great majority of us, they are actively and willfully laboring toward our common recovery from this long illness.

About the potential fruits of this compassionate disposition, Saint Isaac of Syria has written a great deal, including the following, which—you may not be surprised to hear—has me thinking of my sweet Labradors:

> And what is a merciful heart? It is the heart's burn-ing for the sake of the entire creation, for men, for birds, for animals, for demons, and for every created thing; and by the recollection and sight of them the eyes of a merciful man pour forth abun-dant tears. From the strong and vehement mercy that grips his heart and from his great compassion, his heart is humbled and he cannot bear to hear of or to see any injury or the slight suffering of anything in creation. For this reason he offers up tearful prayer continually even for irrational beasts, for the enemies of truth, for those who harm him, that they be protected and receive mercy. And in like manner he even prays for the lowest as a result

of the great compassion which—after the likeness
of God—is poured out beyond measure within his
heart.[28]

The consensus of scriptural witness and of the
broader tradition agrees that by the fact of our
humanity, we are all of us already dwelling in "the
image of God"; the trick lies in our proceeding into
His likeness, wedding our own will to His.

five *complicity*

Behold now, what is so good or so pleasant
As for brothers to dwell together in unity?
—PSALM 132:1

One of the great commonplaces among aggrieved agnostics or atheists is the perennial—if nonetheless rhetorical—question, How can anyone believe in an allegedly loving God who allows the innocent to suffer? It is true that I am neither an atheist nor exactly an agnostic, but in my own way, off and on, I have had occasion to ask much the same question.

As a matter of fact, a poem I composed some years ago—the eleventh section of a twelve-part sequence—still manages to serve up a glimpse of my own, intermittent ambivalence. It first appeared in a chapbook in 1993. The plaintive poem is called "Pain."

No new attempt at apology here:
All suffer, though few suffer anything
like what they deserve.

Still, there are the famous undeserving
whose pain astonishes even the most
unflinching disciples

whose own days have been consumed by hopeless
explanation for that innocent whose torn
face or weeping burns

or ravenous disease says simply no,
not good enough. This is where we must begin:
Incommensurate

pain, nothing you can hope to finger
into exposition, nothing you can
cover up. A fault

—unacceptable and broad as life—gapes
at your feet, and the thin soil you stand
upon is giving way.[29]

As for the persistent inquiry itself—how a loving
God would either cause or allow the continued
suffering of the innocent—it remains a pretty useful
question, if only because it is so quick to reveal
an illusory premise that I am no longer willing to
buy—the premise of individual autonomy.

For one thing, a question like this indicates a
pervasive ignorance regarding how intimately we

are connected to one another, both now and, as I now suspect, *ever*.

It also pays insufficient attention to the extreme freedom that God appears, most often, to insist upon in His creation, from top to bottom.

And both of those phenomena, duly considered, provide a clue about why the discrete occasions of all this suffering aren't exactly God's doing.

Perhaps sooner than later, we will probably want to grapple with God's curious insistence on the radical freedom of creation; but for now, let's attend to the business of how intimately we are connected, one to another. The connection is absolute.

I daresay that if the innocent suffer, they do so because one of us—you or me or some other thug—now or in the past, has set their pain in motion.

And if the innocent continue to suffer, they do so because we have yet to take responsibility for their pain; we have yet to take sufficient responsibility for their relief.

Our failure to appreciate the degree of our own responsibility encourages—and, more often than not, continues to enable—our famous disinterest in those who suffer, allows us a continuing, dim-witted, and blithe condemnation of those in pain or in poverty. In our hearts we know that something has caused their pain and their failure; our broadly continuing failure to see our own hands and hearts in that process keeps us assuming that the afflicted are somehow to blame for their circumstances, shaking our heads as we stand by or, more often, as we turn away, feeling both helpless and—assuming that we're not *completely* dead yet—a little culpable. That faintest whiff of our own culpability is our subtle evidence that there may be hope for us yet.

Dostoevsky's Zosimas has a keen sense of this culpability. "There is only one salvation for you," he says to his gathered brotherhood: "take yourself up, and make yourself responsible for all the sins of men. For indeed it is so, my friends, and the moment you make yourself sincerely responsible for everything and everyone, you will see at once that it is really so, that it is you who are guilty on behalf of all and for all."

And there is an even greater consequence that Zosimas would alert us to: "Whereas by shifting your own laziness and powerlessness onto others, you will end by sharing in Satan's pride and murmuring against God."[30] You might even join the grim chorus of those who cannot believe in a God who would allow such things.

In the midst of his own suffering, even unto death, Elder Zosimas makes clear his sense of this great mystery of our mutual complicity:

> Remember especially, that you cannot be the judge of anyone. For there can be no judge of a criminal on earth until the judge knows that he, too, is a criminal, exactly the same as the one who stands before him, and that he is perhaps most guilty of all for the crime of the one standing before him. When he understands this, then he will be able to judge. However mad that may seem, it is true. For if I myself were righteous, perhaps there would be no criminal standing before me now.[31]

In his book about the life and witness of his own spiritual father, Saint Silouan the Athonite,[32] Archimandrite Sophrony[33]—a modern-day ascetic of the Holy Mountain—further recovers for us this ancient understanding when he writes:

> Sin is committed first of all in the secret depths of the human spirit but its consequences involve the individual as a whole. . . . Sin will, inevitably, pass beyond the boundaries of the sinner's individual life, to burden all humanity and thus affect the fate of the whole world. The sin of our forefather Adam

was not the only sin of cosmic significance. Every
sin, manifest or secret, committed by each one of
us affects the rest of the universe.[34]

My time with the fathers and mothers of the
church has made clear the undeniable truth that
my own sin is not only about me. The general
consensus—spanning a good sixteen hundred
years—would have it that your sin is not only about
you, either. Every choice in our lives that separates us
from communion with God, and every decision that
clouds our awareness of His presence or erodes our
relationships with one another has a profound and
expanding effect—as the proverbial ripples in a pool.
And that effect is to give us precisely, by so choosing,
what we prefer over communion with God, what
we prefer over our cultivating an awareness of His
presence, and over our having healthy relationships
with one another: namely, ourselves alone.

Ourselves alone, it turns out, is an outcome and
a circumstance that must finally be appreciated as
the complete and utter antithesis of our becoming
healthy human persons. The very notion of the Holy
Trinity (in Whose image we are made) should lead
us to suspect that personhood requires relationship,
that genuine personhood depends upon it.

My hope for healing, therefore, lies in my becoming more of a person, and more intimately connected to others. For us to succeed as we are called to succeed, we must all come to share this hope.

Satan himself (should we say *itself*?) proves an interesting and exemplary case in point. In Satan, we have a being that has doggedly opted for isolation, for nonbeing, and for acute (albeit a comically moot) independence. Except for the book of Job—another famous if perplexing study in affliction—we do not find much about Satan in the Scriptures. A good bit of our thinking about the character of Satan has come to us by way of John Milton's epic poem, *Paradise Lost,* rather than from Holy Scripture. That isn't to say the Miltonic construction isn't useful to our thinking; Milton took his theology seriously. One revealing passage occurs in Book IV, where Satan speaks thus:

> So farewell, hope; and with hope farewell, fear;
> Farewell, remorse! all good to me is lost;
> Evil, be thou my good; by thee at least
> Divided empire with Heaven's King I hold,
> By thee, and more than half perhaps will reign;
> As Man ere long, and this new world, shall know.[35]

With a tasty bit of dramatic irony, Milton offers up a Satan who—even in the midst of his profound and strenuous denial of God's authority—fails to notice that his own innovative moral economy (in which God's evil becomes Satan's good) nonetheless depends upon God's having established the prior economy in the first place. With a keen sleight of the poetic hand, evil is revealed as merely a denial of the good, an absence of the good, and nothing of itself—nothing, really, beyond spiteful, *infernal* response.

Early in the seventh century, the beloved Saint Isaac had already come to a comparable conclusion concerning the figure of Satan, and also came to understand the ontological status of sin, of Gehenna, and of death as similarly vexed:

> Sin, Gehenna, and death do not exist at all with God, for they are effects, not substances. Sin is the fruit of free will. There was a time when sin did not exist, and there will be a time when it will not exist. Gehenna is the fruit of sin. At some point in time it had a beginning, but its end is not known. Death, however, is a dispensation of the wisdom of the Creator. It will rule only a short time over nature; then it will be totally abolished. Satan's name derives from

voluntary turning aside from the truth; it is not an indication that he exists as such naturally.[36]

In a his translation of the above, Sebastian Brock puts it even more plainly: " 'Satan' is a name denoting the deviation of the human will from truth; it is not the designation of a natural being."[37]

One might say further that "Satan" is not the name of *natural being,* period. It is the name for that which rejects being, that which is satisfied to become *aberration.* It is necessarily the name for that which, turning away from the natural, the good, and the beautiful—and away from the God whose communion gives life to all things—has turned, instead, toward nothing, nonbeing, toward its own isolation, severance, and death.

So much for Satan.

———

Writing in the fourteenth century, Saint Gregory Palamás made a similar observation regarding the nature of evil: "It should be remembered that no evil thing is evil insofar as it exists, but insofar as it is turned aside from the activity appropriate of it, and thus from the end assigned to this activity."[38]

As both Saint Isaac and Saint Gregory Palamás are eager to establish, while sin is to be understood as nothing of itself, it can be *quite* something in terms of its effects. Admittedly, our particular English noun *sin* can be misleading given that, generally speaking, when we bother to put a name to a thing, we expect that thing to exist. The Greek precursor, *amartía* (literally, "missing the mark"), is a good deal more instructive for our apprehending the status of things; the Greek word's construction, beginning with that familiar *a*—which is to say, beginning with *not*—attends to sin's ontology, its originating energy. It is the *great not*, the infernal *no* to God's eternal *yes*. It is ever and always *mis*taken. *Dissing* the marker, it misses the mark. It is the failure—or the refusal—of *being*, plain and simple.

Those of us who struggle with habitual sins—and we know who we are—are very likely to break our hearts over the business of turning away from those chronic *mark missings*. Our problems with recurring sin, and the more general human problem of being enslaved by sin, is never solved simply by our reject-ing that sin, no matter how many times we try, no matter how strenuously we struggle to reject it.

This is because merely *rejecting* sin—that is, focusing on *not* sinning—is finally just another species of *infernal no*.

"Just say no" is an insufficient principle.

The strongest man or woman in the world is not nearly strong enough to triumph over his or her sin simply by saying *no* to *it*. What we need is the strength-giving grace occasioned by our saying *yes* to *something else*, by our saying *yes*, and *yes*, and *yes*—ceaselessly—to *Someone* else.

It is not our finally *turning away* from sin that frees us from sin's recurrence; rather it is our *turning toward* Christ—and the mystery of our continuing to turn into Him—that puts sin behind us.

One other illustration comes to mind. Orthodox Christians generally observe three fasting seasons during the year besides Great Lent;[39] many also observe most Wednesdays and Fridays as discrete days of fasting throughout the year. These are days when, for the most part, neither meat nor dairy foods are eaten. The tradition is keen to insist that fasting be accompanied by almsgiving. One forgoes expensive foods in favor of the inexpensive, and one is encouraged to share with the poor the money saved by eating on the cheap. Not to put too fine a point on the matter, the tradition teaches us that a fast—or any manner of self-deprivation—that is not accompanied by

some good thing done for another is understood
to be "a Satanic fast."

Forgive my inserting a bit more poetry to bring
home the point. This particular piece is one of a sort
of playful, mostly serious series of poems having to
do with word studies in New Testament Greek; in
this case, the word is *metánoia*.

> Repentance, to be sure,
> but of a species far
> less likely to oblige
> sheepish repetition.

> Repentance, you'll observe
> glibly bears the bent
> of thought revisited,
> and mind's familiar stamp

> —a quaint, half-hearted
> doubleness that couples
> all compunction with a pledge
> of recurrent screw-up.

> The heart's *metánoia*,
> on the other hand, turns
> without regret, turns not
> so much away, as toward,

as if the slow pilgrim
has been surprised to find
that sin is not so bad
as it is a waste of time.[40]

The *good,* on the other hand, is what actually
exists; our long and continuing tradition tells us
that all that is worthwhile is good, and all that is
good is worthwhile. Moreover, all that partakes of
the good is by good's efficacious agency brought into
existence, and is by that selfsame agency kept there.

Regardless of our situations, we are inevitably
partaking of something or other at every moment.
The catch is that we will either partake of *what is,* or
we will partake of *the absence of what is.* We partake
either of life (all that has true being by way of its
connection to God) or of death (all that has opted
to sever that connection).

As we all must have guessed by now, we actually
are what we eat.

six *recovered body*

Then they cried to the Lord in their afflictions,
And He saved them from their distresses;
He sent His Word and healed them,
And delivered them from their corruptions.
—PSALM 106:19–20

As I have labored to indicate through this essay—though you have suspected this business already—our lives are riddled with death.

The good news, which presumably you also already have gathered, is that even this death is potentially infused with life. In fact, this is surely the difference between those of us who are fully awake and those who remain, more or less, sleepwalkers— the substantive difference between the quick and the dead.

For a good while now, this is the sense I have gained regarding that moment in the Nicene Creed when we collectively confess our faith, saying, "He will come again to judge the living and the dead."[41] I no longer think of that creedal proposition as asserting that He is coming to *mete out* life or death, but that in His coming, He will discern and will announce which of those states we have already chosen. He does not condemn us to death, but He informs us if we are dead already.

It may be fair to say, moreover, that while all of humankind continues by grace to derive its very life from God, only some of us happen to notice and thereby to benefit fully from that fact. "For to be carnally minded," Saint Paul writes, "is death, but to be spiritually minded is life and peace" (Rom. 8:6).

Life—no less—with peace in the bargain!

Over the years since my leaving home for college (more precisely, since my belated discovery of the fathers and mothers of the church first led me east), salvation itself has come to mean something large to me, something full—both substantial and immediate.

For the monks on Mount Athos, salvation—or, better, "*being* saved"—does not have to do with a discrete and isolated instant of conversion; it is not a matter of cinching a done deal. The traditional understanding of salvation indicates our moving *toward* and *into* a continuously thickening reality. If you have read C.S. Lewis's beautiful little book *The Great Divorce*, you will have a likely image to accompany this vertiginous prospect of a *thickening reality* and of the human person shifting from airy shadow to illuminated substance.

Salvation is a continuing process of being redeemed; it is our recovery from our chronic separation from God, both *now* and *ever,* and it includes our becoming increasingly aware of Who our God is. Our miraculous salvation has very little to do with the popular notion of "dying and going to heaven," and has far more to do with finally *living,* and with entering the kingdom of God, here and now.

Here again, Archimandrite Sophrony of the Holy Mountain comes to us with keen insight: "The essence of sin consists not in the infringement of ethical standards, but in a falling away from the eternal Divine life for which man was created and to which, by his very nature, he is called."[42] Conversely, the essence of salvation lies in our *leaning into* that eternal divine life, and our thereby being in position to derive endless life from our mystical—but nonetheless palpable—connection with the God Who Is.

The monks and their Orthodox traditions have insisted—from the earliest writings on the matter—that this calling and this salvation is offered to all of humankind, not just to those relatively few who acknowledge membership. Of course, the Orthodox fathers and mothers would be quick to insist that the most trustworthy and most satisfying road to full participation in the saving life of Christ is revealed in the traditional teaching *of* and participation *in* that One, Holy, Orthodox, Catholic, and Apostolic Church; they are also fairly unshakable in the conviction that the One Body— that is to say, Christ's body—is synonymous with that self-same church. We acquire our salvation *through* our partaking of that body, regardless of our meager apprehension of the matter.

Bishop Kallistos Ware famously parses this mystery: "We can say where the Church is; we cannot say where she is not." As our Lord Jesus Christ tells the earnest and anxious Nicodemus, like the wind, the Spirit blows where it wishes.[43]

As I now see it, salvation has come to mean deliverance, and deliverance right now, from the death-in-life routine that we often settle for—the sleepwalking life that I—and maybe you—have often settled for in the past. Saint Isaac, again, offers firm support to this vertiginous phenomenon:

The man who has found love eats and drinks
Christ every day and hour, and hereby is made
immortal. "He that eateth of this bread," [Christ]
says, "which I will give to him, shall not see death
unto eternity." Blessed is he who consumes the
bread of love, which is Jesus! He who eats of love
eats Christ, the God over all. . . . Wherefore, the
man who lives in love reaps the fruit of life from
God, and while yet in this world, he even now
breathes the air of the resurrection.[44]

Inextricably related to this discovery is another
developing sense that while salvation necessarily
happens to persons, it is not to be understood as a
merely personal matter.

I continue to enjoy—and enjoy repeating—the
surprising response that a monk at Simonopetra
gave to a man who—thinking he had come to
evangelize the Holy Mountain—asked the kind
father if Jesus Christ was "his personal savior."

"No," the smiling monk said without hesitation,
"I like to share him."

Thanks to the long-standing tradition that monk
manifests, I have a developing sense that salvation
finally must have to do with all of us, collectively,
and that it must have to do with all else as well—all
of creation, in fact.

It turns out that I am not alone in my thinking so.

My reading in the fathers and the mothers of the church—assisted by my discovery of what I would call rabbinic, midrashic Bible reading[45]—has me thinking that all of creation is implicated in this phenomenon we variously call salvation, redemption, reconciliation. Like the late theologian John Romanides, I suspect that our saving relationship with God is quite specifically "*as* the Body of Christ"; our salvation is not a discrete, individualized, private bargain struck, but comes by way of our continuing participation in divine life, as a *member* of a holy body that is at once both alive and life-giving.[46]

I have many beloved friends, men and women, whom you would recognize immediately as genuinely loving people, exceedingly good people, if you were to spend a day with them. They are, without question, serious, kind, deeply spiritual believers of one stripe or another; they also share an insatiably deep hunger for community, which they try to satisfy with worthwhile activities. They also, oddly enough, share an abiding sense of alienation from the body of Christ, at least as that body is expressed in the media and quite often in their local churches.

Many of them have blithely said—to my very puzzled and grimacing mug—that, while they may be *spiritual,* they are not *religious.* I comprehend the unfortunate distinction being made by their parsing of terms, and that distinction continues to strike me as the result of an insidious and ongoing failure— theirs, ours, and mine.

Be that as it may, somehow or other and *regardless,* these beloved friends must find their way home. They must find a way to a reconnect their faith to their communities and their communities to their faith. They must find a way to reconnect, as it were, the *spirit* with the *body.* Satan, our tradition tells us, looks for any vessel sailing without a fleet, and it seems to me that an individualized, isolated "spirituality" is almost by definition satanic.

I have been relatively late in coming to this myself. In fact, my own difficulty with "fitting in" at the various churches I attended from my high school days through my early thirties had me in the same isolated boat. I went a good—or rather, a decidedly *bad*—ten or so years without a body; I was a severed member, languishing alone. These days, I see more vividly how we are called to work out this perplexing business together, and I see that faith is not something that can be both solitary and healthy. The health and eventual fruitfulness of the severed limb depends utterly upon its being grafted onto the living tree.

This is, in part, what I suspect that Dietrich Bonhoeffer was hoping to reintroduce to his community in *Life Together*, wrestling as he does to reclaim the sacrament of confession. He states matter-of-factly:

> [T]he Christian needs another Christian who speaks God's Word to him. He needs him again and again when he becomes uncertain and discouraged, for by himself he cannot help himself without belying the truth. He needs his brother man as a bearer and proclaimer of the divine word of salvation. He needs his brother solely because of Jesus Christ. The Christ in his own heart is weaker than the Christ in the word of his brother; his own heart is uncertain; his brother's is sure.[47]

His brother's word and heart—in the case of a confessor—are also informed by that most generous of democracies, in which even the allegedly dead have a vote.

Without batting an eye, Bonhoeffer insists that the presence of the brother—or, more to the point, the

presence of *the Christ* borne in that brother's heart—
shores up one's own faith, comforts and assures one's
own trembling heart. It is the fact of their being "two
or [more] . . . gathered together in [Christ's] name"
(Mt. 18:20) that enables their mutual apprehension
of His assuring and unfailing presence.

This may be one of the reasons why, even
among the ruling monasteries of Mount Athos,
the idiorrhythmic (individualized) rule has been
set aside in favor of the more deeply traditional
coenobitic (community) rule; the fathers' lives
in Christ are necessarily *lives together*. Even the
increasingly rare eremite, the desert dweller, in his
bleak and rugged cave at the edge of Katounakía
regularly makes his way to the monastic enclave for
the purpose of liturgical worship and communion.
In the Orthodox tradition, there is no such thing as
solitary communion.

This uncanny gift of a *life together* is not the
property of monastics alone, but is offered to us all.
The more troubling point remains, therefore, that
until such time as each of us claims that gift and
lives into it, the entire body suffers, and we—as
severed members—are inclined to dry up, becoming
deadwood, no good to ourselves or to anyone else.

"Ignorance and sin are characteristic of isolated individuals," writes the Russian priest Father Alexander Elchaninov. "Only in the unity of the Church do we find these defects overcome. Man finds his true self in the Church alone; not in the helplessness of spiritual isolation but in the strength of his communion with his brothers and his Saviour."[48] Elsewhere this same wise priest offers a word of caution: quoting Saint Paul, he observes, "'And when one member suffers, all the members suffer with it' is said of the Church. If we do not feel this, we are not within the Church."[49]

Dwelling somewhere at the heart of this lies the Christian understanding of the human person, an understanding that commences with the conviction that every one of us—of whatever religion or non-religion—is made in the image of God, and that we all continue to bear His divine image, however well or poorly we do so. As the Orthodox like to say, we are all of us *written* as the *icon* of God.

The *One* God is said to exist in *Three* Persons engaged in a single *perichóresis,* a single circling dance, and our familiar—if inexplicable—trope of *Trinity,* is our shared tradition's preferred manner of figuring God Himself as an *essentially* relational being.

The Image-bearing human person is therefore also necessarily a relational being, so much so that for all Christians in the early church—an individual is not considered the same thing as a person; authentic personhood stipulates the communion of one with another.

Simply put, an isolated individual does not a person make.

As for what we call salvation, it is not to be understood simply as an individual or a *future* condition, but as a moment-by-moment, *present* mode of being—even as an ongoing acquisition, a developing realization. This may have been, in part, what Jesus was teaching us when he said, "For indeed, the kingdom of God is within you" (Lk. 17:21). This is what he may have been getting at when he announced, "But I tell you truly, there are some standing here who shall not taste death till they see the kingdom of God" (Lk. 9:27).

Jesus did not misspeak. There were, without question, among his exponentially expanding band of followers, "some standing . . . who would not taste death" before they had witnessed the kingdom of God, had tasted its power, and were already savoring its abundant life, even as they hobbled with the rest of us through the valley of the shadow of death.

According to the fathers, this is a kingdom, a power, a glory, and a quality of life that is potentially no less apprehensible to us now.

"The ladder of the Kingdom," writes Saint Isaac, "is within you, hidden in your soul. Plunge deeply within yourself, away from sin, and there you will find steps by which you will be able to ascend."[50]

Let this admonition mix with a further word regarding the matter from Archimandrite Sophrony:

> What does salvation mean? Do our bodies have to die so that we can enter the kingdom of Christ? How can we develop our capacity to live according to Christ's commandments, according to the Holy Spirit? Only one thing counts: to keep the tension of prayer and of repentance. Then, death will not be a rupture, but a crossing to the Kingdom for which we will have prepared ourselves by communion in the Body and Blood of Christ, by prayer, and by the invocation of His name: "Lord Jesus Christ, our God, have mercy upon me and upon Thy world."[51]

Abba Benjamin of Scetis—one of the most ascetic, if also more obscure, among the desert fathers—is said to have left his spiritual children, as he lay dying, with this provocative paraphrase of Saint Paul's message to the Thessalonians: "If you observe the following, you can be saved, 'Be joyful at all times, pray without ceasing, and give thanks for all things.'"[52] It is not incidental that, even on his deathbed, the loving father remained more concerned with the well-being of his spiritual children than he was with his imminent death.

Here, then, in the lucid words of Abbas Benjamin and Sophrony, I glimpse those who are speaking from *within* the kingdom already. The one who apprehends the reality of God's unfailing presence, the one who sustains ongoing conversation with His Holy Presence, is able to apprehend *all things* and all experiences—the good, the bad, the beautiful, the ugly, our loves *and* our afflictions, even our apparent deaths—as *purposeful*. That blessed pilgrim is able—even through his or her tears—to taste and to see that the Lord is good, that even our pain is remedial, that even our suffering is grace.

Forgive my again getting personal, but my own earlier struggles with a fiery temper have also been mitigated in recent years by an increasing apprehension of God's holy kingdom *here and now*.

Mulling all this over, there was a time when pride had me thinking that every insult, offense, or error had to be corrected, and by me, and immediately.

If someone were to treat me poorly, I made certain he knew about it; if someone unjustly blamed me for any petty thing that went awry, the blame was duly delivered to its rightful owner.

Again, this is all in retrospect, but my subsequent practice of the Jesus Prayer has helped me to deal with these occasions in a very different way. For one thing, the prayer has helped me to trust in God's unfailing presence; for another, this trust—quietly but inexorably—has freed me from my perverse need to let my offender know of his offense.

Over time, the knowledge that God witnessed these occasions with me allowed that anger to be replaced by something more like embarrassment, something like regret. Nowadays I feel complicit in the whole mess, sorry for our mutual human error—and forgiveness goes without saying. The fact that an offender may remain oblivious to that forgiveness is absolutely beside the point.

And so, sure, I too want very much to be saved. These days that means that I want to be saved from what passes for myself. This is because what passes for myself does not always feel quite like the self that is framed in the image of God and is thus unitedwith those around me and is, allegedly, growing with them into His likeness.

I would like to replace this recurrently hamstrung, self-defeating, and mostly isolated *self* with the more promising image: the person in communion with other persons. And while I'm at it, I wouldn't mind undergoing something like a lasting re-*pair* of heart and mind, body, and soul.

As I continue to discover more fully day by day, this journey toward wholeness is not something that one is able to undertake alone. Fellow travelers aren't only a welcome luxury; they are crucial to our bearing our crosses as we seek to follow God.

Of course, we are likely to find that before we can set about healing the rift *between* persons, we have a good bit of interior work ahead of us in terms of repairing and recovering the wholeness *of* our persons, as such.

He leads me beside the still waters.
He restores my soul.

—PSALM 22:2–3

Even in the midst of these, our over-busy, bustling, and distracted lives, even in our seasons of affliction and suffering, our deepest consolation lies in consciously experiencing our mystical membership in the body of Christ. Our hope lies in repairing our chronic separation from that body, and in becoming an increasingly conscious member of that body, partaking of and savoring Christ's ever-presence. We hope to heal the wounds that keep us isolated from Him and from each other, that leave us ineffective, amputated members, and—not to hammer the issue too hard—*failed* disciples of Christ.

Such a healing can very often appear to us as a very beautiful hope; but in my experience we remain susceptible to thinking of it as a very beautiful but unrealistic hope, or one that will have to wait until death trumps our sputtering lives.

It would be far better for us to witness—and for us to bear witness *to*—the miracle of life trumping death, here and now.

Recall, if you will, the extended franchise of our broad democracy that G.K. Chesterton invokes. Think of it as the constituency of holy fathers and mothers (our immortal majority?) who have walked this valley road before us. They have voted, and they insist by proclamation that our desired healing is absolutely possible—even today, just as the Christ has promised. There are some standing here (okay, so you're probably sitting) who will not taste death before they witness the kingdom of God, have tasted its power, have partaken of its abundant life.

Life *Himself,* of course, has already accomplished an absolute trumping of death; we need only to notice, and by our noticing thereafter to participate in His continuing triumph.

That said, our ability to participate in this recovery appears to be dependent upon our tweaking our own, dissipated persons, and healing a concurrent rift in our own, discretely fragmented selves. How, for instance, are we to notice life's triumph over death, here and now, if the human faculty made for apprehending that knowledge is itself out of order, if our instrument is on the blink?

Among a good many other advantages our predecessors in the early church could claim was a more nearly adequate vocabulary. For instance, they were in possession of a number of words that indicated a number of amazing truths. *Nous,*[53] *kardiá,*[54] *népsis,*[55] and *théosis*[56] were among those words that helped to keep the young body focused on the task at hand, the task of healing our shared series of rifts—within themselves, between themselves and others, and between a holy God and a race of creatures that had sorely missed the mark.

Three of those words—*nous, népsis,* and *théosis*—have been all but lost to our contemporary conversation, and the deep significance of another, *kardiá,* which is to say "heart," has been sorely diminished. With these onetime commonplace words enhancing their spiritual conversations, our predecessors were better able to give their attentions to the profound complexity and promise of the human person—another treasure neglected over the centuries.

The import of *nous* has been obscured thanks to a history of not-so-good choices translating that very good Greek word into other languages—initially into Latin and then from Latin into English—that didn't have direct equivalents. What we have received, at best, are half measures. None of them has proven to be sufficiently indicative of the mystery of ourselves.

In most cases, our translators replaced the mysterious noun with something that addresses maybe half of a complicated story.

For instance, when Saint Peter employs his accustomed, muscular language to encourage us: "Gird up the loins of your *mind*" (1 Pet. 1:13), *nous* is the word that is shortchanged, having been replaced with *mind*. When we read in Saint Paul's epistle to the Romans, "And do not be conformed to this world, but be transformed by the renewing of your *mind*, that you may prove what is that good and acceptable and perfect will of God" (Rom. 12:2), the word *mind* is again what we are given in the place of the more suggestive *nous*.

In the above passage from Saint Paul, a good deal of significance appears to be placed upon right thinking—specifically, the renewing of our *minds*—as if by thinking better thoughts, by fine-tuning our theologies, or by undergoing a bit of brain buffing we might find ourselves duly equipped to "prove what is [the] good and acceptable and perfect will of God."

Virtually every time we come across the word *mind* (or, in some cases, *intellect* or *reason*) in an English translation of the New Testament, *nous* is the word being rendered—one might say surrendered.

The greatest danger is that what should be an actively performed faith, a *lived* faith, becomes little more than an idea. When it is most healthy, ours is not a simply propositional faith, but a faith embodied and performed.

Another New Testament word that could benefit from a rigorous appraisal is *kardiá,* offered to us simply as *heart.* Early Christians—taking their lead from Jewish and other Semitic traditions—understood this word as indicating more than the pump in our chests, or a figure for our emotions, feelings, and affections; they understood *kardiá* as the very center of the complex human person, and as the scene of our potential repair.

As our long tradition has figured the matter, the human person is herself/himself something of a trinity. Various writers in that tradition are likely to name our tri-parts variously, but most agree that thanks to the dire severing of our persons from the Triune Persons of our Life-giving God, we have become splintered, or something of a crippled tripod, a triangle that doesn't ring true.

We may be body, soul, and spirit, true enough, but—for most of us—our wholeness and unity remain either troubled or downright fractured. We are compelled toward balance, but we are bent. We hope to be even, but we are at odds—at odds with ourselves, at odds with our constituent bits, and as a result we have become somewhat less than the sum of our parts.

"Gather yourself together in your heart," writes Saint Theophan the Recluse, "and there practice secret meditation. . . . The very seed of spiritual growth," the saint insists, "lies in this inner turning to God. . . . Or, still more briefly, collect yourself and make secret prayer in your heart."[57] On another occasion, Saint Theophan writes, "The Savior commanded us to enter into our closet and there to pray to God the Father in secret. This closet, as interpreted by St. Dimitri of Rostov, means the heart. Consequently, to obey our Lord's commandment, we must pray secretly to God with the mind in the heart."[58]

The "mind in the heart."

The more we read in the fathers and mothers across the early centuries of the church, the more powerfully we come to recognize this formula, this admonition that we might find our prayer lives made fruitful by our descending with our "minds" into our "hearts." This figure, then—of the lucid *nous* descended into the ready *kardiá,* of the mind pressed into the heart—articulates both the mode and locus of our potential re-collection, our much-desired healing; at the very least, it identifies the scene where this reconstitution of our wholeness might begin—the center of the human body, which is nonetheless the temple of the Holy Spirit.

Split as we are, we think with our minds and we feel with our bodies. Imagine a habit of prayer that serves to marry both faculties together. Imagine a covert organ at the core of our beings that—duly apprehended, duly cleansed, and duly inspirited— is able to reconnect those severed capacities within ourselves, so that our internal struggle between the appetites of the body and the varied solipsisms of the mind resolves, finds peace in likely collaboration.

A finer sense of things is occasioned by Bishop Kallistos Ware's depiction of the *nous* as "the intellective aptitude of the heart." In this fortunate collision of *mind-talk* and *body-talk*, we glimpse something of what the figure of the *nous* descended into the *kardiá* performs; the *nous* inhabited *kardiá* becomes the place where mind and body meet, a place where their long-standing severance might be healed, their half-measures made whole, a place where the human split is potentially re-paired.

The faculty occasioned by the mind's descent into the heart is also the organ by which we apprehend God's presence as more than an idea, and as more than a passing sensation. The severed mind can help us to the idea of God, and the severed body can provide us with a sensation of His touch; but the noetic center of a healed, triune person offers something more lasting and more satisfying than either—*felt knowledge* of His love and communication with His constant presence.

I have written elsewhere of my conversations with two very wise fathers during my first few pilgrimages to the Holy Mountain. In the midst of my struggle to discover some continuity for my sputtering prayer life, I daresay that God led me to a place where I could hear precisely what I needed to hear.

In the first case, a father at one monastery helped me to see that prayer was itself an ongoing struggle; he likened the matter to that of Jacob's wrestling with the angel of the Lord, and he helped me to glimpse that even the pain of that struggle was to be recognized as a blessing. "You have to plead with Him to meet you here," he said with a gesture to his heart. "And when he arrives, you must hold onto Him, and not let go.

"Like Jacob," he said, "you must hold on to Him. And like Jacob," he said, "you will be wounded. Like Jacob, you must say, 'I will not let You go unless you bless me,' and then the wound, the tender hip thereafter, the blessing.

"He is everything," the father continued, "and ever-present. He is never not here," he said, once more touching his heart, "but when you plead to know He is here, and when He answers you, and helps you to meet Him here, you will be wounded by that meeting. The wound will help you know, and that is the blessing."

Some months later, as I spoke with a father at another monastery, much of this mystery was confirmed. "It is not you who prays," he told me. "This is why you must listen. You must learn that it is God who prays. When you descend into your heart, it is God you find, already praying in you."

———

Recovering a sense of *nous* and a more profound sense of *kardiá* will better equip us for the journey ahead. As for *népsis* and *théosis,* the recovery of these similarly illuminating terms may provide some very helpful insights into what it is we are to accomplish in this, the often puzzling meantime of our lives. *Népsis* can be considered as watchfulness, sobriety, interior attention, and it is this discipline of *népsis* that is understood by the fathers and mothers to be essential to our *théosis*—to our *becoming like Him,* our becoming holy.

As I recognize in my own, none-too-exemplary experience, sin happens when one pretty much agrees to it, when one acquiesces to it. Sin, which clouds the *nous* and hardens the heart, is committed by our—that is, by *my*—failing to be watchful, sober, or sufficiently attentive to the effects of what I think or say or do. The fathers almost uniformly distinguish between an unavoidable, momentary, if not-so-expedient thought (*logismós*)[59] and sin itself (*amartía*).[60]

The provocation to sin only becomes sin when we fail in our watchfulness and fail in our efforts to elude it. An inexpedient thought becomes sin when we turn toward it, and certainly becomes sin when we settle in to savor it.

"My son, give heed to my word," the writer of the Hebrew Proverbs exhorts, "and incline your ear to my words,

> . . . That your fountains may not fail you;
> Guard them in your heart;
> For they are life to those who find them
> And healing for all their flesh.
> Keep your heart with all watchfulness,
> For from these words are the issues of life.
> (Prov. 4:19–22)

"That your fountains may not fail you, guard them in your heart."

Developing this discipline of *népsis,* of watchfulness, teaches us increasingly to guard our hearts from every careless slip into temptation, keeps us from missing the mark, and spares us from squandering whatever spiritual development we may have accomplished. With *népsis,* we avoid our chronic sins that would have us repeatedly starting again from zero.

The *mind descended into the heart,* then, describes where and how we meet Him. *Watchfulness* indicates how we keep that meeting place uncorrupted. And *théosis* reveals how we might apprehend our journey to *Christ-like-ness,* a condition that will gain for us the kingdom of heaven, here on earth. Over time—resulting from what Brother Lawrence[61] has characterized as "the practice of the presence of God"—these meetings become a way of life, and they become the source of our freedom from happenstance, our freedom to face any occasion, any insult, or any affliction with the consoling apprehension of God's being *with* us.

Moreover, the *mind-in-the-heart*—the establishment of the *noetic heart*—also creates the organ by which we finally are able to meet our brothers and sisters, the organ by which strangers are recognized as holy messengers, and the means by which we hope, finally, to realize that whatsoever we do (or fail to do) to the least of these, we necessarily do (or fail to do) to Christ Himself.

As Christ prayed for us, in what our common tradition recognizes as "the high priestly prayer," the prayer He prayed in the garden of Gethsemane "on the night when He was betrayed, or rather when He gave Himself up for the life of the world":[62]

That they all may be one, as You, Father, are in Me,
and I in You; that they also may be one in Us, that
the world may believe that You sent Me. And the
glory which You gave Me I have given them, that
they may be one just as We are one: I in them, and
You in Me; that they may be made perfect in one,
and that the world may know that You have sent
Me, and have loved them as You have loved Me.
(Jn. 17:21–23)

Which means, of course, that we are loved utterly,
but just as the cup was not taken from Him, neither
are we likely to skirt suffering. As Saint Paul avers,
God "did not spare His own Son, but delivered
Him up for us all" (Rom. 8:32).

Oddly enough, our own descents into suffering
may turn out to be the occasions in which we—
imitating His unique and appalling descent—come
to know Him all the more intimately.

eight *what is lacking*

My soul is exceedingly sorrowful, even to death.
Stay here and watch with Me.
—MATTHEW 26:38

During the past dozen years or so—in my (God-willing) middle years—I have developed a healthy taste for ambiguity. One of the reasons I enjoy poetry, for instance, is that a good poem insists that a reader learn to honor ambiguity, that he learn to collaborate with a poem's suggestive possibilities, that she accept the challenge of being a comaker of meaning. That is to say, a great poem—even a pretty good one—isn't ever *done* saying what it has to say.

Ambiguity in a literary text, then, is a helpful clue to a reader that the story doesn't end with a single reading, and a compelling clue to the reader that she must assist in the telling and the retelling. This goes for ambiguity, in general, ambiguity in life.

And it goes for various flavors of uncertainty.

And for perplexity, to boot.

I have begun to discover how perplexity is not such a bad disposition to cultivate, considering. Perplexity is, at the very least, preferable to any array of clear, comprehensible, and *mistaken* certainties.

In fact, acknowledging our uncertainties in the face of perplexing circumstances may prove finally to be a very good thing, even something of a gift. More often than not, these uncertainties can lead us into acknowledging, as well, the point where human understanding fails—as it inevitably must do. And our noticing that point can, thereafter, nudge us into realizing that the actual—the True— is immeasurably immense. Whatever the truth turns out to be, it is ever and always *necessarily* far more than we can know.

Just as—recalling the words of Saint Isaac— knowledge of "our weakness" is the beginning of all that is good and beautiful, this knowledge of "the limits of our knowledge" can—in and of itself— bear witness of the inexhaustible enormity of our God. It can give to us a comforting assurance that even if *we* are inevitably constrained by our limitations, our God and His reality continue to extend far beyond what we can make of them. In a deeply quiet and calming way, this offers something like a subliminal proof that we didn't simply make up this whole story.

I have already alluded to midrashim, the *searching out* of Scripture; it is but one specific practice of our deeper tradition that has always savored the inexhaustibility of scriptural revelation. For the wise rabbis poring over their Bible scrolls, perplexity is understood to be the key to subsequent revelation; for them—as it should probably be for us—the Scriptures are understood to be capable of assisting us to an ever deeper relationship with our God. Their midrashic method has been to "search out" the difficult passages—the utterly perplexing ones—trusting that, if those passages appear to trouble their assumptions, it is because their assumptions needed work. Their vision was due for revision.

Among the wealth of scriptural perplexities made available to us in Saint Paul's serial epistles, perhaps the most perplexing occurs in the first chapter of the saint's letter to the Colossian church. In verse 24, we come across a very odd observation as Saint Paul speaks of his own experiences of suffering for his brethren and for their common faith: "I now rejoice in my sufferings for you, and fill up in my flesh what is lacking[63] in the afflictions of Christ, for the sake of His body, which is the church" (Col. 1:24).

Had you noticed that before?

What—one cannot help but wonder—could possibly be lacking in the afflictions of Christ? What could be deficient?

This is known in the business as "a hard saying," "a *dark* saying," and it is not likely to settle well with those—perhaps *especially* with those—who prefer to take their Scriptures neat, or very literally. It is hardly less a dark saying, as well, even for those of us who embrace a more figurative, metaphorical sense of the Scriptures as the continuing "witness" to the Revelation—the actual Revelation being Christ Himself.

While we're having recourse to a relatively old-school custom of doing our theology by way of "chapter and verse" exegesis, we may as well throw into the mix a complementary observation offered by Saint Peter: "Beloved," Saint Peter writes, "do not think it strange concerning the fiery trial which is to try you, as though some strange thing happened to you; but rejoice to the extent that *you partake of Christ's sufferings*, that when His glory is revealed, you may also be glad with exceeding joy."[64]

The notion that Christ's sufferings lacked anything may strike some of us as borderline heresy; the idea is a least counterintuitive. The Greek word yielding the odd "lacking" in our English translations of Saint Paul's letter—*isterímata*[65]—is not likely to increase our comfort. I have seen it translated, here and there, as "deficiency"—which strikes me as even worse—but I'm thinking that its grammatical indication of a *future* matter can give us a bit more of a clue. A more likely translation seems to me to be *what is yet to be done*.

In any case, this does not exactly solve our puzzle. One is very likely still to ask, *what* is yet to be done?

What is it that Saint Paul and the rest of us are expected to supply?

Could it be *ourselves*?

The very heart of an efficacious faith, it seems to me now, is bound up precisely in our—watchfully—living into this mystery of what appears to be God's continuing desire for collaboration between Himself and His creation.

From Adam's naming of the animals through each successive patriarch, prophet, and holy man or woman, God has shown a predilection for working *with* His people, as opposed to simply working *on* them. God is intent, generation after generation, on finding one or more of us to suffer the chore with Him. They may or may not always be the best specimens—Moses, Abraham, Lot, David, etc.—but their success is inevitably bound up with their complying with His will, and colluding with it. We find instances of this dynamic collaboration throughout our biblical texts and throughout their surrounding traditions.

One chief instance that comes to mind is illustrated in the Gospel dialogue that accompanies the event we call the Annunciation—that most curious exchange between the Archangel Gabriel and the Theotokos[66]—and I glimpse in that fascinating give-and-take the Holy Mother's *necessary* concurrence with the angelic messenger's announcement. The angel reveals to her the message from on high, and she replies, "Behold the maidservant of the Lord! Let it be to me according to your word" (Lk. 1:38).

The point is, she said *yes* to God's messenger. One despairs to think what would have become of us if she had said *no*.

I used to think that the popular notion of *synergy* came into usage out of a trendy, pop culture, new age fuzziness. However, various forms of its Greek antecedent—*synergía*[67]—crop up throughout Scripture, from the Septuagint through the Epistles. The patriarchs, matriarchs, prophets, apostles, and potentially, the rest of us are all figured as coworkers—with God and with each other. Even our worship, our liturgy—*liturgía*[68]—is understood as our being participant in that efficacious and ongoing "work."

The God-created world is an exceedingly wild place. Its weathers and its very makeup—its famously cranky geology—remain notoriously unpredictable. Bad things happen to good people; good things happen to bad. And even setting aside the simply bad, there is also no shortage of downright evil, from which the good do not appear to be uniformly protected. "For He makes the sun rise on the evil and on the good, and sends rain on the just and on the unjust" (Mt. 5:45).

What kind of God *is* this?

Whether or not you think the world was initially created as the shaky sphere it is—a notoriously unstable crust skidding over a roiling swirl of molten rock—there's no arguing that it isn't something of a crapshoot now. Earthquakes, hurricanes, tornadoes, landslides, volcanic eruptions, tsunamis, famine, flood—take your pick. And lest we forget the human hand in our crapshoot's wealth of crap, we must remember to add to that wild mix our own pathological history of aggression, murder, war, and genocide.

And *where*, exactly, is our God in all of this?

———

Well, the story goes that He has descended into the very thick of it.

The story goes that He remains in the very thick of it.

In mystical *synergía*, He collaborates with His Body, now and ever. In appalling condescension, He remains *Emmanuel*, God with us. Whereas we had brought only death and brokenness to that mix, He has brought life and wholeness.

We may recall that some among the first-century Jews in Jerusalem—in particular those who believed Jesus to be the Messiah—were both surprised and disappointed that He didn't "redeem Israel" in quite the way they had assumed He would. The thief being crucified beside Christ was not simply baiting Jesus when he asked of Him, "If you are the Christ, save yourself and us"; he was probably thinking that if this bloodied man hanging beside him were truly God's anointed, then any reasonable, self-respecting Christ would do just that—save Himself.

The Christ, in any case, had bigger fish to fry—enough to satisfy the multitudes.

Which was why He did not *save* Himself, but rather *gave* Himself.

He did not come simply to rid the Jews of the oppressive Romans any more than He came to trump the other oppressive circumstances that His oddly beloved creatures have continued to construct for themselves and others. On the contrary, He came to suffer the results of those cosmic bad choices with us, and by so doing to both show us how we might survive them and to enable our survival—in Himself.

That is to say, He did not come here to undo our choices, but to move through them victoriously, and to show us how we might likewise move. He did not come to eclipse us, or to overrule our persons. On the contrary, He came to endow our persons with the self-same unending life.

———

What, then, *has yet to be done*? What—so far as
you are concerned—is the nature of this odd-seem-
ing *isterímata* that gives Saint Paul cause to rejoice
even in the midst of suffering?

You'll probably have to tell me.

I suspect that, just as each of us is unique in the
eyes of our God Who loves us, each of us also will
find a unique remedy for our separation from Him.
Each of us will discover—and either will bear or
will shirk—a unique cross.

What the fathers and mothers of the church have
taught me is that inevitably each of us will, in one or
in a number of ways, partake of Christ's suffering,
and that these experiences will help us to apprehend
all the more how we are both joined to Him and
how we are joined to each other.

We may well have occasion to ask—as Christ
Himself asked—that the cup be taken away, but we
will fare far better if that request is followed by "yet
not my will, but Your will be done." We will fare far
better if, like the Theotokos, we answer the call of the
messenger, saying, "Behold the servant of the Lord.
Let it be done to me according to your word."

As I write this, the Holy, Orthodox, Catholic, and
Apostolic Church—that would be the *one* mystical

body of which we are all members, like it or not—is entering the season we call Great Lent.

Admittedly, some of us may be doing so more deliberately than others, but to one extent or another we are all entering the preparation for the Feast of Feasts—Great and Holy Pascha—what many of us grew up calling Easter.

Here, at the almost end of my baggy essay, I feel that it is time for an analogy.

———

Last night at Saint Luke parish, we celebrated Forgiveness Vespers, and today is Clean Monday, the beginning of our penitential journey. For the next seven weeks or so, observant folks will, for the most part, abstain from eating meat and dairy products; certain well-trained athletes of prayer will forgo oil as well. We will do what we can to give greater assistance to those in need, and we will make our way to church more often for the "supporting services" that the church has established to help its divers members through this period.

It is a season of fasting and of almsgiving, of denying our own appetites as we attend more consciously to the needs of others—and this, even as we descend into serious interior work.

It is—in some sense—a self-imposed affliction, a deliberate suffering; it is—in some sense—a death.

It is, nonetheless, a death attended by hope, a death that anticipates new life.

The Greeks have a word for this strange mixture of dispositions that characterizes the spirit of Great Lent; they call it *harmolype,* and in English, the notion is spoken of as "bright sadness" or "sorrowful joy."

The late Father Alexander Schmemann has written of the complex character of Lenten observance, thus:

> For many, if not for the majority of Orthodox Christians, Lent consists of a limited number of formal, predominantly negative, rules and prescriptions: abstention from certain food, dancing, perhaps movies. Such is the degree of our alienation from the real spirit of the Church that it is almost impossible for us to understand that there is "something else" in Lent—something without which all these prescriptions lose much of their meaning. This "something else" can best be described as an "atmosphere," a "climate" into which one enters, as first of all a state of mind, soul, and spirit, which for seven weeks permeates our entire life. Let us stress once more that the

purpose of Lent is not to force on us a few formal obligations, but to "soften" our heart so that it may open itself to the realities of the spirit, to experience the hidden "thirst and hunger" for communion with God.[69]

Father Schmemann writes of how a "quiet sadness" permeates the Lenten services themselves; "vestments are dark, the services are longer than usual and more monotonous, there is almost no movement." He observes that despite the alternating readings and chants, "nothing seems to happen." And so, he acknowledges, we stand for a very long time in this quiet, this sadness, this monotony.

"But then we begin to realize that this very length and monotony are needed if we are to experience the secret and at first unnoticeable 'action' of the service in us. Little by little, we begin to understand, or rather to feel, that this sadness is indeed 'bright,' that a mysterious transformation is about to take place in us."

Moving through the sadness, we glimpse the joy. We feel its effects on us and feel how it changes us. We are thereby led to a place where noises, distractions, and false importance of the street—of our dissipated lives—finally "have no access—a place where they have no power."[70]

Similarly, then, in those seasons of our afflictions—those trials in our lives that we do not choose but press *through*—a stillness, a calm, and a hope become available to us; they are a stillness, a calm, and a hope that must be acquired slowly, because—as Father Schmemann says of our joy in Lent—"our fallen nature has lost the ability to accede there naturally."[71]

So, we are obliged to recover this wisdom slowly, bit by bit. And I will leave the final bit to the amazing Simone Weil. She writes: "The extreme greatness of Christianity lies in the fact that it does not seek a supernatural remedy for suffering, but a supernatural use for it."[72]

———

May our afflictions be few, but may we learn not to squander them.

We have but one yellow Labrador left. The beloved Rita is nearly eleven years old, white-faced, and lumpy from head to wagging rump. In recent weeks I've noticed that she is having trouble getting up and down the stairs, and even needs help getting up on our bed.

As I was walking up our driveway this afternoon, coming home earlier than usual, I could hear her in the house—she was howling.

Sneaking a look through the front window on my way to open the door, I saw our last dog sitting on the living room couch, her head raised, nose to the ceiling, pouring out one long soulful note into the empty air.

Now and ever, Lord Jesus Christ, Son of God, have mercy on me.

a c k n o w l e d g m e n t s

The poem "After Great Pain, a Formal Feeling Comes" by Emily Dickinson that appears on page 9: Reprinted by permission of the publishers and the Trustees of Amherst College from *The Poems of Emily Dickinson*, Thomas H. Johnson, ed., Cambridge, Mass.: The Belknap Press of Harvard University Press, Copyright © 1951, 1955, 1979, 1983 by the President and Fellows of Harvard College.

The poem "Gravy" by Raymond Carver that appears on page 21: Copyright © 1989 by the Estate of Raymond Carver. Used by permission of Grove/Atlantic, Inc.

The poem "Musée des Beaux Arts" by W.H. Auden that appears on pages 22–23: Copyright © 1940 & renewed 1968 by W.H. Auden, from *Collected Poems* by W.H. Auden. Used by permission of Random House, Inc.

1. Simone Weil (1909–43) did not live long, but she did manage to live deeply, with profound sympathy for the impoverished and for victims of aggression. She died of tuberculosis, following years of self-imposed poverty. A brilliant woman, she observed, "The intelligent man who is proud of his intelligence is like the condemned man who is proud of his cell."

2. Simone Weil, *Gravity & Grace* (Lincoln: University of Nebraska Press, 1997), 132.

3. If we are not so lucky, or if our hearts and minds have already been—by long-determined habit—confined solely to the realm of the apparent, we are probably going to opt instead for some serious antidepressants.

4. Emily Dickinson, "After Great Pain, a Formal Feeling Comes." For the source of this poem, please see the Acknowledgments on page 117.

5. Borrowing their vocabulary from the Greek philosophers, the fathers and the mothers of the early church have given us, among other insightful riches, the word *apátheia,* which (free of the unfortunate connotations of our latter day *apathy*) denotes a calm interest, an unshakable faith in the good, or at least in the potential good that is latent in all that comes about.

6. *The Syriac Fathers on Prayer and the Spiritual Life*, trans. Sebastian Brock (Kalamazoo, MI: Cistercian Publications, 1987), 250.

7. *Daily Readings with St. Isaac of Syria* (Springfield, IL: Templegate Publishers, 1990), 50.

8. Raymond Carver, "Gravy," in *A New Path to the Waterfall* (New York: Atlantic Monthly Press, 1989), 118.

9. W.H. Auden, "Musée de Beaux Arts," in *Collected Poems*, ed. Edward Mendelson (New York: Vintage International, 1991), 179.

10. George Steiner, *Real Presences* (Chicago: University of Chicago Press, 1989), 3–4.

11. George Steiner, "Preface to the Second Edition," in *Tolstoy or Dostoevsky* (New Haven, CT: Yale University Press, 1996), xiv–xv.

12. Saint Symeon the New Theologian, *Hymns of Divine Love*, trans. George A. Maloney, (Denville, NJ: Dimension Books, 1976), 168–69.

13. Galatians 3:27 (emphasis mine).

14. The word *atonement* was coined by William Tyndale, who sought to offer a more complete English gesture for the Hebrew concept of *kaphar*—"to cover over." The word is an attempt to indicate the dual aspect of Christ's incarnation and sacrifice: the remission of sin and reconciliation of humankind to God.

15. The cleanliness code of Leviticus is also impli-
    cated in Matthew 5:48, "Therefore you shall be
    perfect, just as your Father in heaven is perfect."
16. "Ἅγιοι ἔσεσθε, ὅτι εγώ ἅγιός [εἰμι]."
17. My new rule of thumb: whenever my own
    contemporary disposition suggests to me that
    I might modify an ancient tradition, evade
    a difficult Scripture, or revise a long-held
    understanding of the church, I've decided
    such innovation should be preceded by careful
    thought and no small amount of prayer. I'm
    finally beginning to see that, most often, *I* am
    what needs changing, not the tradition.
18. *Wounded by Love: The Life and Wisdom of Elder
    Porphyrios*, trans. John Raffan (Limni, Evia,
    Greece: Denise Harvey, 2003), 132.
19. G.K. Chesterton, *Orthodoxy* (San Francisco:
    Ignatius Press, 1995), 52–53.
20. Against the odds, and against the diminishments
    of the faith occasioned by such regrettable
    dichotomies as *faith* versus *works,* we must
    insist that ours is not finally a *propositional*
    faith, but is necessarily a *performed* faith, an
    incarnated faith. Let's call it an *embodied* faith.
    Either we come to perform that faith with our
    lives or we continue simply to talk about it, to
    kid ourselves about what goats we are. And yes,
    the pun is intended. Point of fact: the pun is
    always intended.

21. Dostoevky's fictional Zosimas is generally understood to be based upon the very real starets (elder) Saint Ambrose of Optima (1812–91†), who served for thirty years as abbot and starets of the Optima monastery, and the founder of the Shamordino convent.

22. Isaac of Nineveh (Isaac the Syrian), *"The Second Part,"* Ch. IV–XLI trans. Sebastian Brock (Leuven: Peeters, 1995), 172.

23. Note that Grigory—who had known and continued to know great affliction—found comfort in the witness of the book of Job, that quintessential narrative of human suffering.

24. Fyodor Dostoevsky, *The Brothers Karamazov*, trans. Richard Pevear and Larissa Volokhonsky (New York: Farrar, Straus and Giroux, 1990), 96.

25. Ibid., 74–75.

26. Ibid., 319.

27. Ibid., 318.

28. *The Ascetical Homilies of Saint Isaac the Syrian* (Boston: Holy Transfiguration Monastery, 1984), 344–45.

29. Scott Cairns, "Pain," from "Disciplinary Treatises," in *Figures for the Ghost* (Athens: University of Georgia Press, 1994), 40.

30. *The Brothers Karamazov*, 320.

31. Ibid., 320–21.

32. Saint Silouan the Athonite (1866–1938†) was born Simeon Ivanovich Antonov. With the blessing of Saint John of Kronstadt, he entered the Holy Mountain, becoming a monk at the Russian monastery Saint Panteleimon. From the Holy Theotokos he received the gift of unceasing prayer, and thereafter saw a vision of Christ in uncreated light. When that initial grace was withdrawn, he struggled with profound grief and temptation for a period of fifteen years, after which he received from Christ the teaching, "Keep thy mind in hell, and despair not."

33. The Athonite father Sophrony, previously known as Sergei Symeonovich Sakharov, was born in Moscow in 1896. Appalled by his own apostasy, he entered the Holy Mountain and the monastery of Saint Panteleimon in 1925, were he came into contact with Saint Silouan.

34. Archimandrite Sophrony, *St. Silouan the Athonite* (Crestwood, NY: SVS Press, 1991), 31.

35. John Milton, *Paradise Lost* (New York: Appleton-Century-Crofts, 1933), Book IV, lines 108–13, p. 212.

36. *Ascetical Homilies of Saint Isaac the Syrian*, 133.

37. *The Wisdom of Saint Isaac the Syrian*, trans. Sebastian Brock (Oxford: SLG Press, 1997), 5.

38. Saint Gregory Palamás, *The Triads* (Mahwah, NJ: Paulist Press, 1983), 28.

39. There are generally four fasting periods each year: Great Lent (which is in preparation for Easter), the Nativity Fast (which is in preparation for Christmas), and two shorter, two-week periods, the Apostles' Fast and the Dormition Fast, in June and August, respectively.

40. Scott Cairns, "Adventures in New Testament Greek: *Metánoia*," in *Compass of Affection: Poems New & Selected* (Brewster, MA: Paraclete Press, 2006), 93.

41. Και πάλιω ερχόμενον μετά δόξης κρίναι ζώντας και νεκρούς.

42. Archimandrite Sophrony, *St. Silouan the Athonite*, 31.

43. John 3:8.

44. *Ascetical Homilies of Saint Isaac the Syrian*, 224.

45. Something of a precursor to the Christian concept of *lectio divina*, the Jewish practice of "searching out" the subtle meanings of a holy text is based upon the understanding that these sacred words—being the "name of G-d"—are inexhaustible in their potential to instruct us.

46. Andrew J. Sopko, *Prophet of Roman Orthodoxy: The Theology of John Romanides* (Dewdney, BC: Synaxis Press, 1998), 12–13.

47. Dietrich Bonhoeffer, *Life Together* (New York: Harper & Row, 1954), 23.

48. Alexander Elchaninov, *The Diary of a Russian Priest* (London: Faber & Faber, 1967), 87.

49. Ibid., 124.

50. *Ascetical Homilies of Saint Isaac the Syrian*, 11.

51. Archimandrite Sophrony, *Words of Life* (Essex, UK: Patriarchal Stavropegic Monastery of St. John the Baptist, 1996), 15.

52. *The Sayings of the Desert Fathers*, trans. Benedicta Ward, (Kalamazoo, MI: Cistercian Publications, 1975), 4.

53. νους

54. καρδιά

55. νέπσις

56. θέωσις

57. *The Art of Prayer: An Orthodox Anthology*, comp. Igumen Chariton of Valamo (London: Faber & Faber, 1997), 77–79.

58. Ibid., 53.

59. λογισμός

60. αμαρτία

61. Brother Lawrence was a seventeenth-century lay brother of the Discalced Carmelite Priory in Paris. His meditation on the life of prayer, *The Practice of the Presence of God,* has become an invaluable Christian classic.

62. From the Divine Liturgy of Saint John Chrysostom, the Eucharistic service used most often in the Eastern Orthodox Church.

63. υστερήματα, the shortage, deficiency, or, more nearly, what is yet to be done.
64. 1 Peter 4:12–13 (emphasis mine).
65. υστερήματα
66. Among Eastern Christians, *Theotokos*—the God-bearer—is the preferred name for the Virgin Mary.
67. συνεργεία
68. η λειτουργία
69. Alexander Schmemann, *Great Lent: Journey to Pascha* (Crestwood, NY: St. Vladimir's Seminary Press, 1996), 31.
70. Ibid., 32.
71. Ibid., 33.
72. Weil, *Gravity & Grace*, 132.

About Paraclete Press

who we are

Paraclete Press is a publisher of books, recordings, and DVDs on Christian spirituality. Our publishing represents a full expression of Christian belief and practice—from Catholic to Evangelical, from Protestant to Orthodox.

We are the publishing arm of the Community of Jesus, an ecumenical monastic community in the Benedictine tradition. As such, we are uniquely positioned in the marketplace without connection to a large corporation and with informal relationships to many branches and denominations of faith.

what we are doing

b o o k s—Paraclete publishes books that show the richness and depth of what it means to be Christian. Although Benedictine spirituality is at the heart of all that we do, we publish books that reflect the Christian experience across many cultures, time periods, and houses of worship. We publish books that nourish the vibrant life of the church and its people—books about spiritual practice, formation, history, ideas, and customs.

We have several different series, including the best-selling Living Library, Paraclete Essentials, and Paraclete Giants series of classic texts in contemporary English; A Voice from the Monastery—men and women monastics writing about living a spiritual life today; award-winning literary faith fiction and poetry; and the Active Prayer Series that brings creativity and liveliness to any life of prayer.

r e c o r d i n g s—From Gregorian chant to contemporary American choral works, our music recordings celebrate sacred choral music through the centuries. Paraclete distributes the recordings of the internationally acclaimed choir Gloriæ Dei Cantores, praised for their "rapt and fathomless spiritual intensity" by *American Record Guide,* and the Gloriæ Dei Cantores Schola, which specializes in the study and performance of Gregorian chant. Paraclete is also the exclusive North American distributor of the recordings of the Monastic Choir of St. Peter's Abbey in Solesmes, France, long considered to be a leading authority on Gregorian chant.

D V D s—Our DVDs offer spiritual help, healing, and biblical guidance for life issues: grief and loss, marriage, forgiveness, anger management, facing death, and spiritual formation.

Learn more about us at our Web site:
www.paracletepress.com,
or call us toll-free at 1-800-451-5006